North Platte's KEITH BLACKLEDGE

Lessons from a Community Journalist

Carol Lomicky with Chuck Salestrom

THE
History
PRESS

Published by The History Press
Charleston, SC
www.historypress.com

First published 2021

Manufactured in the United States

ISBN 9781467148047

Library of Congress Control Number: 2020948439

Notice: The information in this book is true and complete to the best of our knowledge. It is offered without guarantee on the part of the author or The History Press. The author and The History Press disclaim all liability in connection with the use of this book.

For Mary Ann.

CONTENTS

ACKNOWLEDGEMENTS

L ong before I became involved in this project, Keith Blackledge's friend and colleague Chuck Salestrom fell "victim" to one of Keith's lunch invitations, and together they began video recording interviews with North Platte community leaders and others connected to the editor's work and life. As their relationship deepened, Chuck realized that there was a story that needed to be told. Thank you, Chuck, for bringing me into this project.

Lucky for me, Keith kept everything—newspaper articles, his editorials and columns, background information, personal papers and correspondence—some kept in tall filing cabinets at the North Platte Public Library and others in boxes and files at the Lincoln County Historical Museum. Thanks to the library staff—particularly Kaycee Anderson, who for several years tolerated my presence in the conference room as I read, organized and indexed the materials.

The fun part was conducting the interviews—most face to face, some on the phone, others via e-mail and still others through old-fashioned letter writing. I am deeply indebted to Keith's wife, Mary Ann, who spent hours with me and provided me access to family mementos, scrapbooks and photographs. Invaluable also were the conversations with Keith's sons, his colleagues, his friends and the people who worked with him at the *Telegraph*.

Thanks go to the Mid-Nebraska Community Foundation for the grant that helped fund my research; Rhonda Seacrest and Sharron Hollen for their generosity; George Hipple, photographer extraordinaire; and digital wizard Jessica Epting. Others whose moral support cannot be overstated include families, especially the spouses Tom Lomicky and Kristi Salestrom; the folks at the *North Platte Telegraph*, who patiently answered questions and retrieved stuff; the many friends and colleagues whose interest and encouragement really kept the project moving forward; and the team at The History Press, especially Chad Rhoad and Ryan Finn. I appreciate each and every one of you.

PROLOGUE

It has been my goal to edit a newspaper that would seem like a friend to the people who bought it. In that, as in all these other things, it is not always possible to succeed. Much of the news is unpleasant. I haven't been able to do anything about that.
—*Keith Blackledge*[1]

The editor, imposing despite his small stature, stood by his office door and gazed out at the newsroom of the *North Platte Telegraph*. It was just before noon on Wednesday, October, 22, 1975. Reporters clacked away on typewriters; another ripped wire service stories coming over the teletype machine; and a few, using rubber cement and a brush, glued pages of their typewritten stories together. Back in the composing area—just within eyeshot of the editor—typeset galleys ran through the wax machine. It wouldn't be long before the tedious paste-up process would begin—placing each story, headline and pre-scanned photo on the page as specified on the dummy sheets. It was all hustle and bustle to meet the early-afternoon deadline for the day's press run. Meanwhile, every news staffer was fully aware of the presence of Keith Blackledge, the editor they both respected and feared. To which part of the daily routine would be his focus this time, they wondered. Was he looking to make sure no one was idle as phones rang, as reporters and photographers perused film strip negatives, as the copy editor returned stories to reporters for rewrites or fact checks? It was difficult to tell, for the slanting rays of sun bathing the newsroom in filtered light obscured the editor's piercing brown eyes, already partially concealed behind his owl-like spectacles.

As Blackledge continued to stand by his office door, the mostly young staffers knew that it wouldn't be long before the editor would begin a slow stroll through the newsroom. Years later, Dan Moser, former *Telegraph* reporter/editor, remembered this not infrequent occurrence:[2]

> *Keith would just stand at the door of his office; everyone was aware of it when he was there. He'd just stand there looking out—no one was sure who he was looking at. Then he would start "sharking." He would roam around the newsroom—not talking, just roaming.*[3]

And so, on this particular late morning in the fall of 1975, Blackledge began to shark as his news team cast furtive eyes toward one another while hunkering down over desktops and typewriters, some in exaggerated busyness. In those days, newsrooms were without partitioned workspaces, making it more difficult for them to hide.

As Blackledge strolled through the newsroom, he registered almost automatically what appeared to be utter chaos as reporters, editors, photographers, darkroom technicians and page make-up designers prepared yet another daily edition for press time. There sat Bill Eddy, the assistant editor, phone tucked under his chin, rapidly typing an obituary on a call from one of the Adam and Swanson Funeral Home directors.[4] Handwritten pages of reporter Sharron Hollen's interview notes covered the top of her desk.[5] Hollen is good, Blackledge thought—that rare journalist who is both reporter and writer. At least sports editor John Martinez wouldn't be in for several more hours.[6] His and Hollen's antics can distract, although, Blackledge admitted to himself, they're in good fun and often amusing.

As Blackledge meandered the newsroom that day, he was deep in thought. The last few nights had been late, beginning on Saturday, when Eddy had shown up at his house to alert the editor, who'd already turned in for the night, about those gruesome murders over in Sutherland and the panic it was causing in North Platte because it was rumored a gunman was on the loose. Eddy's doing a good job, Blackledge mused. He'd put together the news team to begin gathering information that very night. Thankfully, the suspect, after hiding in a field all night, had been apprehended early Sunday morning. Monday's front-page stories and photos of the crime and arraignment of Erwin Charles Simants, the accused, indicated how much significant time and space the paper likely would be devoting to the coverage. Tuesday night was also a late one while first awaiting the election returns and then celebrating the voters' approval of a hard-fought school bond issue. Add to this the ominous threat to local media created during a closed-door session in the courtroom last night, when the Lincoln County judge considered issuing a gag order on the press before Simants's preliminary hearing. Blackledge questioned the sense it made to allow journalists into the hearing while also prohibiting them from reporting any details of the crime. The newspaper certainly could be facing a challenging set of circumstances, Blackledge thought, but the staff, though young, is capable. No doubt the newspaper's own editorial cartoonist, local mail carrier Carl Bieber, would find the impending dilemma fodder for a cartoon or two.[7]

As the editor roamed the newsroom, he continued to reflect. Two building completions and subsequent ribbon cuttings this year had culminated extensive heated debate: first, the new McDonald-Belton Building of Mid-Plains Community College was dedicated in February, then the Great Plains Medical Center building in August. Too bad the Wild West World Musical couldn't make a go of it, Blackledge thought, and to give up the Nebraska Midland Railroad to Stuhr Museum in Grand Island was unconscionable. Certainly the fate of the carousel at Cody Park remains anyone's guess. And who knows if that dubious proposal to locate a fountain out by Interstate 80, will ever become reality. Blackledge shrugged.

Decades later, Blackledge told an interviewer that "1975 was a big year. We dedicated the hospital, we had a $10 million dollar school bond election that passed in '75—and I really worked on that school bond issue—the Simants case was in '75."[8] Indeed, 1975 was the year Blackledge was named editor and director of community affairs and, a short time later, editor and vice-president of the *Telegraph*.

By 1975, the business of putting out a newspaper was quite different than it had been when Blackledge graduated from the University of Missouri College of Journalism and sharpened his journalism skills at the North Platte *Daily Telegraph-Bulletin*, where from 1952 to 1959 he served as reporter, sports editor, city editor and managing editor. As Blackledge recalled:

> *In 1952 reporters and editors typically worked on ancient beat-up typewriters handed down from the business side. Stories were typed on copy paper, edited with a dark pencil, and sent to a linotype operator who typed them all over again.*[9]

Lured by big-city journalism, Blackledge left the *Telegraph* in 1959 for positions first in Fort Lauderdale/Miami, Florida, and then Dayton, Ohio. He returned to the North Platte paper in 1967 to head the news editorial operations as technology was beginning to change the industry. Certainly by 1975, the electronic revolution had caught up with the *Telegraph*. "In the early 1970s I found myself working at an electric typewriter. Fingers used to pounding out a story had to learn to touch lightly. But even old editors can learn some new tricks," Blackledge remembered. Soon Video Display Terminals (VDTs) would replace the typewriters. "It wasn't long before a computer felt 'right,' an electric typewriter awkward, and a manual typewriter impossible."[10]

The years had brought change to the town too. When Blackledge first came to North Platte in the early 1950s, there was no interstate, no postsecondary school and no development south of the South Platte River. There were two small and aging hospitals. There was a single two-lane viaduct over the railroad tracks at Jeffers. The newspaper office was on Fifth Street across from Sears and down a block from the White Horse Bar, sometimes called the newsroom annex.[11]

In 1975 alone, besides the new Great Plains Medical Center and the new Community College south campus facility, other major city improvements included the recreation–swimming pool complex, several new plant facilities and warehouses, a new branch building for the McDonald State Bank and two new restaurant franchises. A few years earlier, the new Union Pacific Diesel Repair Shop had opened, and the NEBRASKAland Days Buffalo Bill Rodeo was being performed in the new Wild West Arena.

But not all of the development would be for the good, as history would teach and Blackledge would caution. Beginning in 1973, the demolition of the Union Pacific depot, which housed the North Platte Canteen during World War II, marked the beginning of redevelopment initiatives that would negatively affect North Platte's downtown.[12]

Certainly, a new $4 million mall was drawing shoppers from throughout the region, yet empty storefronts downtown continued to increase despite the $692,000 federal urban renewal program that built a modern retail multiplex at the northeast corner of Sixth and Dewey to replace the historic but dilapidated Neville Building, which was demolished in 1975. One year later, a row of commercial buildings on East Front Street was razed. Despite public concern over the demolition of historic structures, the trend would continue into the 1990s.[13] Blackledge fought each of them.

Returning now to that autumn day in 1975, as the *Telegraph* presses were about to roll, Blackledge made one last pass through the newsroom before ambling back to his office. Time to put into words his idea for tomorrow's editorial. He began to type:

> *The free press–fair trial controversy which has occupied the attention of newsmen and courts and attorneys is an endless dialogue over the past decade or so has visited itself upon North Platte and Lincoln County. We did not ask for it. We do not enjoy it. We would just as soon it would go away. But it won't.*[14]

And it didn't go away, not even after the U.S. Supreme Court in 1976 handed the press a significant victory in *Nebraska Press Association v. Stuart* by finding the restrictions placed on the media to be unconstitutional. The free press/fair trial conflict that had been unleashed by Simants's heinous crimes would continue to plague the newspaper and the town for years to come.

Blackledge could be considered a "mythical community newspaper editor...a hero of American Democracy whose image was burnished by American popular culture's glorification of newspapers in the 1970s."[15] Yet his career extended well into the last half of the twentieth century, when the newspaper industry was hit by a tsunami of change, including shrinking circulations and advertising revenues, along with the onslaught of new technologies that would alter forever the ways in which news is both produced and consumed. Nonetheless, Blackledge, who served as editor of the *Telegraph* from 1967 to 1992, remained the prototypical community journalist. He worked mostly behind the scenes to promote and better the town he loved, while in his editorials and columns he praised, scolded, cajoled, teased and encouraged *Telegraph* readers. Blackledge was the motivating force behind community projects small and large: the beautification scheme that had citizens on their hands and knees planting and tending the curbside marigold plots throughout the town, the campaign that merged two small hospitals into a leading regional medical center, the effort to establish the Mid-Nebraska Community Foundation and many more.

He continued to write his weekly column, "Your Town and Mine," until his death in 2010. "Keith always knew he wanted to be a small-town editor," said his widow, Mary Ann.[16] North Platte would prove to be the perfect place for him.

Chapter 1

HIS CALLING WAS JOURNALISM

A journalist must be so imbued with courage, integrity, humility, wisdom and a sense of justice that he will not be cowed by threats nor cajoled by flattery. He must ever resist the temptation to regard himself as God's appointed oracle; he must dedicate his life to learning. And he must possess such an incorruptible sense of justice that he will never use his position or his influence to protect a close friend nor to attack a personal enemy.[17]

Keith Lester Blackledge was born on November 29, 1926, in Sheridan, Wyoming, the first son of Victor and Isla (Polly) Blackledge. The boy learned about newspapering from his father, who following graduation with a journalism degree from Kansas State University went to work for the *Sheridan Post Enterprise* in Wyoming. The senior Blackledge, who was born on June 3, 1900, later quit his job as advertising salesman at the paper to begin his own printing company in Sheridan; however, the Depression soon put him out of business. He then took a position as advertising manager at the *Scottsbluff Star-Herald*, a paper he would eventually co-own.[18] Although Blackledge's father worked in advertising for most of his newspaper career, he also wrote a weekly humorous column created in a folksy ranch cowhand style. When Keith's father took the advertising job at the newspaper and the family moved to Scottsbluff, Keith was nearly four.

Blackledge's mother, Isla Falkenstien, was born on April 16, 1901, in Kansas. Isla met her future husband, Victor, at age fifteen at the Baptist Church in Onaga, Kansas, where Victor's father, James, served as pastor. Blackledge's mother also attended Kansas State University. The couple married in Sheridan after Victor was employed at the newspaper. Victor preferred the name Polly to Isla, and eventually friends and most family would know her only by that name.

In a column written years later, Keith Blackledge described his mother while reminiscing about the birth of his granddaughter:

> *She is the tiny infant who from the first time I saw her reminded me of my mother. I hadn't believed a new baby could look like anything but a new baby. But there was something about her that echoed the quiet intelligence and gentle humor of her great-grandmother.*[19]

In the family history Keith wrote for his three grown sons, he remembered how proud he was of his father at the *Star-Herald* and sensed that his father was "a man of importance."[20] Indeed, Victor was elected to a four-year term on the Scottsbluff City Council in 1948, during which time he also served as mayor. The newspaper had endorsed his candidacy, but after he was elected, to avoid the appearance of conflict of interest, the paper did not accept any paid business with the city throughout his term.

The young Keith Blackledge learned to love and respect the English language from his mother, Polly, whom he called a stickler for the correct spoken and written word.[21] He said that his own pickiness about matters of word choice and grammar throughout his years as an editor were a reflection of his mother's training—training that influenced Keith's younger brother, Walter, too.

Walter McKinley Blackledge was born in Scottsbluff on July 31, 1931. "I remember when I was little, Dad and Mom would read the funny papers to me, being careful to correct the grammar as they read. We were brought up to value correct English and good expression," he said.[22]

Victor Blackledge. *Blackledge Collection.*

In his "Your Town and Mine" columns published in the *North Platte Telegraph* throughout

Polly Blackledge with sons Keith (in uniform) and Walter. *Blackledge Collection.*

the years, Blackledge provided glimpses of his childhood and school days. For example, first love in first grade:

> *A teacher was my first love. Real love. Let's get married as soon as I get a little older kind of love. A $2, heart-shaped box of valentine candy kind of love. She was beautiful beyond words, with a gracious manner and gentle voice. I fought for the honor of staying after school and cleaning erasers. Can you remember what you learned in the first grade? Neither can I. But I can remember how I loved.*[23]

Blackledge said that he liked English but hated mathematics. When he was threatened with being held back for a year for refusing to learn the multiplication tables, a much-appreciated fifth-grade teacher came to the rescue:

> *Name and face both forgotten, she is remembered nevertheless for having resolved that I would not slide by any longer without really learning the multiplication tables. An Einstein she did not create. But at least she prevented a case of mathematical illiteracy from reaching junior high in that condition.*[24]

In the family history, Blackledge admitted:

> *I should have been an excellent student. My parents and most of my teachers thought I should be. I was not. In most classes I just tried to get by. I dreaded being typed as a brain. In my mind, it seemed that doing well in school meant being a social outcast.*[25]

But despite all efforts to the contrary, the boy excelled in English and penmanship in elementary school:

> *I did quite well at Palmer Method penmanship. Winning the awards given out each year. But in the final year, I had trouble with one teacher, who apparently saw that while I was getting the results called for, I was not using the right technique. No doubt this tendency to shortcut the process contributed to my terrible penmanship later.*[26]

Blackledge also experienced early—and curious—forays into journalism. In 1937, the eleven-year-old discovered a racing pigeon wedged in the crossbars of the city water tower near his home in Scottsbluff. With the help of his dad, the *Scottsbluff Star-Herald* and the Associated Press (AP), it was learned that the pigeon was a racer that had become lost while on a flight from Douglas, Wyoming, and Denver. The bird was returned to its happy owner. The young Blackledge's reward: four registered homing pigeons, plus news stories in the local paper and the AP. Blackledge said later that the experience taught him that journalism is a way to get things done.

Then there was the failed attempt at storytelling photography. With best friend Gene Chase, and using Blackledge's old Kodak Brownie camera, the boys planned to capture a series of photos of a cat eating a mouse to sell to *Life* magazine. Problem was, the animals kept getting away. As Blackledge remembered:

> *The first thing we discovered is that a cat does not linger over his food. The mouse was gone before we had a chance to snap the picture. Well, there were plenty of mice. On the second or third try, I stepped on the mouse's tail to try to slow the process. The cat ate just as fast, and separated the mouse from its tail, still under the toe of my shoe. We finally did get our sequence, and had the film developed at Downey's studio. It was a pretty good series of pictures of a mouse disappearing in stages. Only when we saw the pictures though did we realize we had a major production problem. Somewhere in between "takes," we had switched cats. The mice all looked alike, but the cats didn't. We never did send the sequence to *Life*.[27]*

In 2005, Blackledge recounted the photography experiment for *Telegraph* readers: "The old editor came to understand later that staging a phony sequence was not ethical journalism, to say nothing of the moral issue of mice abuse. The cats were happy though."[28]

The young Blackledge had better luck with his Brownie by taking a twilight photo of the Scotts Bluff National Monument. A local photography studio selected the shot as "Picture of the Week," and Blackledge was awarded a one-dollar cash prize. The best part: an enlargement of the photo was displayed in Downey's main street window in Scottsbluff.

At age sixteen, Blackledge had his own paper route. Delivering the *Star-Herald* to subscribers on the bicycle he called Archie, Blackledge soon perfected both the fold and the hold of the newspaper so he seldom had to leave the seat of his bike:

> *By holding the paper at the top corner of the open fold, you could sail it from the sidewalk to the porch. A good throw was one that landed right in front*

of the screen door. A superior throw was one in which the paper landed in front of the screen door and opened up as it hit so the subscriber could read the front page headlines as he bent over to pick it up. We bragged we could do that at will, but I think it was probably more often a lucky accident.[29]

Paper route duties also included door-to-door collections from subscribers in those days. For reasons unclear to Blackledge, one of his customers, local dentist Dr. R.V. Hull, insisted the boy collect only on Saturday mornings and not at the Hull residence, but rather at the dentist's downtown third-floor office. Blackledge said he got the feeling the Doc enjoyed making him climb the steep, long stairway to his office.[30] Unbeknownst to either of them at the time, the dentist would become the paperboy's father-in-law in 1949.

By high school, Blackledge was gravitating toward journalism, while continuing to eschew math and science. As younger brother Walter joked, "In high school I remember some of the teachers expressing some doubt about having another Blackledge in class."[31]

Still, some forty years later, Blackledge remembered a few of his teachers with fondness and gratitude—Nellie Barron, his Scottsbluff High School algebra teacher, for example:

I had systematically resisted every form of mathematics from multiplication tables on. But I learned algebra. To say that she ruled by fear is not exactly accurate. There was some fear involved, no doubt, but mostly the source of her authority was simply the recognition that she was in charge. She was a plump, matronly woman with a backbone of steel and a look in her eyes that brooked no rebellion, no nonsense, no carelessness. The most incorrigible of us did our homework for Nellie Barron's class. You might fake it in every other subject, but not with her. In class, nobody slept, nobody talked out of turn, everybody paid attention.[32]

Then there was his first high school journalism teacher, whom he described as "one who cared and encouraged an awkward sophomore."[33]

The teacher Blackledge had in sophomore English also made a lasting impression:

For most of the semester we did not use a textbook. Instead, we read and talked about John G. Neihardt's epic poems of the West, "The Song of Hugh Glass" and "The Song of Three Friends." I was a rotten student most of the time. But these were stories—good stories with action and drama, heroes and villains. The poet's way of telling made them hard to read at first, but after a while most of us began to get the sense of rhythm and it became easier. I found myself actually enjoying English class.[34]

As Blackledge told his sons, "It was the first time I realized poetry could be used to tell a good story."[35]

Later, when he was a student at the University of Missouri, one of Blackledge's favorite classes would be taught by the Nebraska Poet Laureate himself, John G. Neihardt.[36] "Anyone who knew John G. had to believe there was something special about being a poet. It could make a little man stand tall. It could make an old man seem young."[37]

In 1943, in the middle of his junior year at Scottsbluff High School, Blackledge and his family moved to Los Angeles, California, where Keith's father was stationed with a coast artillery unit in the U.S. Army. The Scottsbluff house was sold, and along with his mother and brother, he moved to a sixth-floor efficiency apartment in Los Angeles overlooking MacArthur Park. Now a junior at Belmont High School in Los Angeles, Blackledge took a journalism class and found a home with the school newspaper. But it wasn't without a snag: the prim gray-haired journalism teacher "had worn out her capacity for caring and inspiring, but still was tough enough to give an F to a classroom rebel who deserved it."[38] To receive his first—and only—failing grade might have crushed the aspirations of the budding journalist right then and there had not other students talked Blackledge into coming back his senior year. So it was back to the school paper and the senior journalism class, advised and taught by the plump and matronly Frances Hov:

> *She was a homely, middle-aged lady. One hand was deformed by arthritis and nearly useless. But she had a great warmth and love for her students.... She wanted so much for you to do well, that you could not help but try to do your best. I can't remember that she taught the high school student senior of long ago anything about how to write. But she made him write. And that taught him a great deal. Words in the journalism text were not matters to be learned for a test, but principles to guide your life and conduct. The student newspaper was not an extracurricular activity, but a serious and exciting enterprise. No less significant in that time and place than the Los Angeles Times.*[39]

When prizes (purchased by Ms. Hov) were awarded at the end of the school year, Blackledge received, for most inches printed, a little book of short stories and poetry edited by American author and commentator Alexander Woollcott. Blackledge said that he read and re-read parts of that book many times over the years. He carried it with him in the army, and he still prized the book in his later years.

Blackledge continued to squeak by in his math courses at Belmont High. Once he simply got lucky by landing in a class taught by a geometry teacher whom Blackledge figured was not much interested in geometry. "If you couldn't solve a problem on a test, he would allow you to write a poem instead," Blackledge recalled, adding, "I got through geometry on short verse."[40]

Blackledge once described himself as small and slow, but he didn't let that stop him. He loved to play sports. In Scottsbluff, he went out for the high school football team:

> As it turned out, I was a lousy football player.... We had a freshman team, and I was way down the line of reserves. When I got to be a sophomore I was on the fourth or fifth string of the reserve team. If you didn't make the varsity, you were called a "scrub." We played a few "scrub" games against reserves from other schools. Even for those, the coach never called me off the bench.[41]

But every August, Blackledge, hot and miserable in helmet and pads, was there with the rest of the team when football practice started. In 1983 and well into middle age by then, Blackledge recalled his time as a bench-warmer in response to a rash of letters to the editor from parents angry because their children were not getting enough playing time in the games:

> I genuinely loved football for itself, or at least the idea of football. I loved to put on the shoes and the pads with the feeling of strength and power and protection they gave. I even loved the pain and sweat of calisthenics, and the technical points of blocking and tackling and running plays. More than that, I loved the vision of myself helmeted and padded and making glorious, game saving tackles. In team sports it is inescapable that some people will have to sit on the bench while others play. Very often there are more people who do not play than there are who do play. Sometimes this is a more real disappointment to the parents than it is to the person who is sitting on the bench.[42]

But being a scrub who warmed the bench for the Scottsbluff team only stoked the fire. In his final year of high school in Los Angeles, Blackledge made the team. A losing season, yes, but there were two good games in which the little lineman contributed. "The way I played had seemed to make a difference to the whole team," Blackledge said. "It was a lesson that served me well all my life. Whatever my role in an activity was, if I really got into it and did my best, I could make a difference."[43]

An episode in his physical education class at Belmont High provided another lifelong lesson. In testing students' speeds going once around the 440-yard track, Blackledge had the misfortune of being matched against the school track star:

> *I think I was about halfway around the track when he crossed the finish line. For some reason, I didn't follow my inclination to ease up and pretend I didn't care, but kept chugging away with the best effort I could muster. Jeers from the classmates/spectators turned to cheers.*[44]

Here's what he said he learned that day: "Not to be embarrassed by unfair comparisons, and to keep going no matter what. Sometimes I forget that lesson. When I do remember, it has served well in many non-athletic endeavors."[45]

In addition to high school football, Blackledge was on the basketball and tennis teams in junior college; he played football, tennis and basketball and bowled in the military; and he played intramural football for his fraternity at the University of Missouri.

Several early work experiences helped to propel Blackledge toward a career in journalism. Blackledge has described two jobs in particular in columns and correspondences over the years. In 1943, the summer between his junior and senior years of high school, Blackledge was employed by the U.S. Forest Service in Yosemite National Park, where, in an effort to eradicate a disease fatal to white pine trees, he worked on one of the blister rust control crews. Living in tents that housed about a half-dozen boys, crews were hauled by trucks to work sites, where, with pickaxes and sturdy shoes, workers dug up the gooseberry bushes on which the fungus grew. "The gooseberry bushes were in rough terrain. We had to walk through thick brush with sharp pine needles that could puncture the leather of your boots."[46] Blackledge noted that although the job helped prepare him for the military, "the work was hard, the food sparse—and pretty bad—and there wasn't much dollar gain."[47]

In 1946, after military service in the Philippines, Blackledge returned home and got a job at a trucking company in Scottsbluff. "That was where I got some experience moving furniture and other heavy things. It helped me realize how much I wanted to get a college education and a job that didn't involve heavy lifting."[48]

When he graduated from Belmont High School in 1944, Blackledge received the Journalism Honor Plaque for his sports and general news reporting for the school's weekly paper. The seventeen-year-old also was named an honorary life member of the Southern California High School Press Association. But journalism would have to wait.

In 1944, the expectation was that young men would enlist in the military; thus, Blackledge, after acceptance into the Army Specialized Training Reserve Program, headed to Oregon State College in Corvallis. With the promise of completing two semesters of college in six months and a uniform, Blackledge expected to see combat.

In 1944, Blackledge joined the Army Specialized Training Program at Oregon State College in Corvallis. *Blackledge Collection.*

He scraped by in physics and chemistry, did respectably in English…and experienced prejudice firsthand. Blackledge became friends with the group of young men who shared the same dormitory floor. However, among them were a few students with whom Blackledge had numerous arguments because of their support for Hitler. When the return address on one of Blackledge's letters from his cousin Phil Falkenstien was noticed, rumor started that Blackledge was a Jew. Ostracized from the group, Blackledge refused to rebut the charge, and even when he found the words "Blackledge is a Jew" carved on the back of one of the classroom chairs, he held his silence. "To have denied it would have been to show the same prejudice myself," he said, adding that the experience helped him to gain an understanding of how it felt to be persecuted.[49]

On January 22, 1945, Blackledge was processed into active duty at Fort Leavenworth, Kansas, and then went on to basic training at Camp Fannin near Tyler, Texas. In early August 1945 came advanced infantry training at a camp in Alabama; however, a few weeks into what was to have been a seven-week stint, the war was ending. One month later, Blackledge arrived in the Philippines, where "there was a scramble to find assignments for infantrymen, no longer needed as infantrymen," Blackledge said. "Some with a little college on our records were picked for office jobs."[50] Blackledge landed a position shuffling paperwork at Base M, Headquarters Company,

In the Philippines. Blackledge (*right*) and his friend "Lewis from Missouri." *Blackledge Collection.*

as supplies were moved about the islands. He later was assigned to supervise a junkyard of military equipment.[51]

For a time, Blackledge also volunteered to work part time on the base radio station. "It involved flipping records and giving the call letters and time of day periodically. I was not very good at keeping track of the time or the things I was supposed to say," he said regarding what might be considered his only brush with journalism during his two-year hitch with the U.S. Army.[52]

According to his discharge records, Blackledge left the Philippines on September 23, 1946, and arrived back in the United States on October 14, 1946.

During his own army years, Blackledge never stopped at the North Platte Canteen, which from December 25, 1941, until April 1, 1946, served free food and midwestern generosity at the Union Pacific depot to more than 6 million service men and women traveling the troop trains during the war. In 1995, Blackledge took a commemorative ride from North Platte to Omaha on the Victory '95 troop train, which jostled the editor's memories of train rides and his military experience:

> *So I missed the North Platte Canteen....But that was OK. I missed getting shot at, too. After all that great infantry training, I ended up relieving an eager-to-go-home 1941 draftee at a quartermaster supply base in the Philippines after the shooting was over. Which improved my chances of living long enough to ride one more troop train 50 years later and rubbing elbows with real heroes who did real fighting in that war. It was by far the best train ride I can remember.*[53]

Although after graduating from college and pursuing his own newspaper career, Blackledge would never again live in Scottsbluff, Nebraska, much of his writing is infused with fond memories of the town. One could even say that the "Blackledge street" was Second Avenue, where the family lived in houses at nos. 2015, 1503 and 2623—all in plain sight of the water tower and park where he and his friends played as boys.

In 1979, when the North Platte City Council, in a controversial move, voted to relocate animals from the Cody Park Storyland Zoo to Scottsbluff's Riverside Park and Zoo, the towns' two newspaper editors had some fun over the controversy. In his editorial "letter" to Daryl Hall of the *Star-Herald*, Blackledge wrote:

> *Our city sent your city this week two wolves, two foxes, one coyote and one badger. I'm sorry we didn't have a partridge in a pear tree. It would have given the whole thing a more musical ring....I hope your mayor and city council and park director get along better with our animals than our city officials did. It is not that our city doesn't like animals. It is just that somehow these animals got to taking more city government time than almost anything else.*[54]

The Scottsbluff newspaper editor responded in kind:

> *Why shouldn't your former animals like it out here in the Panhandle, where the climate is much milder, the humidity considerably less, and the citizens love their zoo animals? The mayor and city council and park director (and city manager) wouldn't dare eliminate the zoo, for the animals probably are more popular than they are. Not only do we have wolves, foxes, coyotes and badgers, but we have lions, tigers, leopards, buffalo, assorted deer, llamas,*

yaks, goats, a camel, assorted monkeys, several chimps, an ape, geese, ducks, peacocks, javelina and—in the children's zoo—there is a turkey and chickens, raccoons, pigs, baby goats, and a "safe" porcupine....I'm not sure, but I might have also noted a partridge in a pear tree, but on the other hand, it might have been a crow in a cottonwood.[55]

And with that, the editor extended the invitation, "Please, Keith, anytime, you're back in the hometown of your pink-cheeked youth, or whenever any other North Platters are out this way, plan to visit all of our animals."[56]

Whether Blackledge ever took up the Scottsbluff editor's offer to visit Riverside Zoo is unknown; however, Hall and Blackledge remained friendly competitors throughout their newspaper careers.

Chapter 2

A NEWSPAPERMAN IN THE MAKING

I am hell-bent on being a newspaper writin' man, even if I have forgotten my
English lessons to such an extent that I hardly know how to punctuate my name
any more....I think that I have the raw material necessary to make a newspaper
man but it is going to take an awful lot of work to produce a finished product.
For that reason, I would like to get into as good a school as possible taking into
account my dubious high school record.
—Keith Blackledge[57]

After his discharge from the army in 1946, Blackledge spent a few
weeks visiting friends and family in California and Oregon before
returning to Scottsbluff. He took a passenger train from Los Angeles
to Cheyenne, Wyoming, and, impatient for the connection to western
Nebraska, hitchhiked the dusty roads home. Too late that fall to enroll in
college, he landed a job with a local trucking company. He also returned
to the *Scottsbluff Star-Herald*, where he worked in the bindery department
and drove a truck delivering newspapers to communities east of town.
Regarding the work he performed that autumn, he said, "It motivated me
even more to get a college education."[58]

Blackledge once told his father that going to the local junior college
"seemed like about the worst fate that could befall me"; however, he soon
began to see things differently. "It might be a good idea to pick up the
fundamentals of an education right in Scottsbluff where I'd also have the
advantage of getting to spend a year or two at home," he reasoned.[59]

Early in 1947, he enrolled in second-semester courses at Scottsbluff Junior College, where he excelled—even acing beginning chemistry. He was editor of the college newspaper and the yearbook, *The Panhandle*. Soon he would meet his future bride, another journalism student, Jo Ann Hull, the local dentist's daughter.

Remembering the courtship, Blackledge said that he and Jo Ann first double-dated—he was paired with Louise, a shy, quiet, willowy blonde who danced like a stick, and Jo Ann's date was Blackledge's friend LeRoy. Jo Ann kept the conversation going and was a good dancer. "Next time I felt like a date, I took Jo out myself," Blackledge said. "That ended my friendship with LeRoy."[60]

Soon Blackledge and Jo were dating steadily, and in the fall of 1948, both enrolled at the University of Missouri in the Columbia School of Journalism. Blackledge joined the Kappa Alpha fraternity and took classes to meet the requirements for acceptance in the university's journalism school.

Blackledge also signed up for the air force armament program with the Reserve Officer Training Corps, completing the advanced ROTC program during his first two years at MU. He spent six weeks in the summer of 1948 in an ROTC camp at Lowry Air Force Base in Denver.[61] In the spring of 1949, Blackledge began taking journalism courses. But ROTC duties, part-time jobs and fraternity life proved to be a strain. To make matters worse, Blackledge was disappointed with the beginning reporting course. "The class had large labs and meaningless assignments. At one time my 'beat' was the local bus depot where I was supposed to hang around and find stories of important people coming and going."[62] Instead of class, Blackledge played pinball at a local haunt until the two graduate students who ran the lab caught him. At their urging, the truant student made the effort and squeaked by—but with barely a passing grade.

In the meantime, Blackledge had given his fraternity pin to Jo, which in those days was a precursor to a formal engagement. On July 1, 1949, under the headline "Wedding Date Announced" on the "Nuptial News" page of the paper, the engagement of Jo Ann Hull and Keith Blackledge was proclaimed in the *Scottsbluff Star-Herald*. Two smiling mug shots of the couple accompanied the article.

They were married on August 21, 1949, in a 2:00 p.m. ceremony at the Scottsbluff First Methodist Church. Brother Walter was best man, while Jo's eighty-two-year-old grandfather, Reverend W.W. Hull of Edgar, Nebraska, performed the nuptials. The newlyweds honeymooned in Cheyenne, Wyoming, and then went on to Snowy Range for several more nights. En route home, they skipped lunch to have enough money for gas.[63]

Nuptial News

Vol. I. No. 1   Friday, July 1, 1949, Scottsbluff, Nebraska   4 Pages

Wedding Date Announced

War Veteran Is Victim of Co-ed System

Two and one-half years ago, Keith Blackledge unsuspectingly returned from the rigors of the army to enroll in Scottsbluff Junior College. Here he was to face the wiles of the opposite sex in the co-educational system.

Perhaps, Keith wasn't quite awake and not his usual wary self in that chemistry class at 8 a. m. As he entered that class, little did he suspect what fate had in store for him.

Jo Hull, a member of that chemistry class, noticed the arrival of an unsuspecting male and began immed-

(Continued on Page 4)

Jo and Keith Set Aug. 21 as Glad Day

Very few people were surprised and none disappointed when it was announced today that Jo Hull and Keith Blackledge have chosen Sunday, August 21, 1949 as their wedding date. The announcement was made at an informal party attended by a few close friends of the bride-elect.

Jo and Keith have been "keeping company" since Scottsbluff Junior College days. They made an informal announcement of their engagement in a fraternity pinning ceremony, October 2, 1948 at Columbia, Mo.

The bride-to-be announced that the ceremony will be held at the First Methodist Church in Scottsbluff, at 2 p. m. August 21, with the Reverend W. W. Hull officiating. Guests will include the relatives and close friends of the two families.

Attendants to Miss Hull at this ceremony will be: Mrs. William Brennen, Miss Georganne Hulse ,and Miss Barbara Wheeler, all of Scottsbluff; Mrs. A. C. Carpenter, Coronado, Calif.; Mrs. H. F. Benn, Lincoln, Neb.; Mrs. H. J. Thomas, Boulder, Colo.; and Miss Margaret Kupilik, Longmont, Colo.

Walter M. Blackledge,

brother of Keith, will act as best man.

Nothing contradictory to these plans has been heard from Keith who is now in summer school session at the University of Missouri.

Rev. W. W. Hull To Tie the Knot

"This ceremony will be my 187th such service in the last 52 years," said the Rev. W. W. Hull at an interview a few weeks ago.

The Rev. W. W. Hull is the grandfather of Jo Ann Hull and will travel to Scottsbluff from his home in Edgar, Neb., for the ceremony. He has been a guest in the home of his son, Dr. R. V. Hull, several times previously but this is his first visit in this official capacity.

The engagement announcement in the *Scottsbluff Star-Herald,* July 1, 1949. Keith Blackledge and Jo Hull were married on August 21, 1949. *Blackledge Collection.*

Back at the University of Missouri the next fall, together the newlyweds took the magazine writing class. Blackledge sold two stories he wrote for the class to the *St. Louis Post-Dispatch* and another article about a popular popcorn hangout off MU campus to *The Popcorn Merchandiser*. He got an A in the class and began to think of himself as a freelance writer.

On a rainy Friday afternoon on June 9, 1950, Blackledge and his bride graduated with journalism degrees from the University of Missouri. President Harry S Truman, the commencement speaker, congratulated the graduates for having proven "they are able to think for themselves, and to work hard day by day to reach a truly worthwhile goal."[64] Blackledge's plan was to start on a graduate degree in the fall at MU. "I probably was secretly terrified at the idea of having to get a real job," he said.[65] But by fall, Blackledge had cooled on the graduate school idea. He went half-heartedly through registration, went home for lunch one day and found the telegram ordering him for active military service. "What a relief," he declared.[66] Once again, journalism was put on hold.

On August 12, 1950, Blackledge, who was among thousands of reservists being called up in response to the turbulence between the two Koreas, reported for duty at Chanute Field, Illinois. Subsequent orders returned him to Lowry Air Force Base in Denver, where he first worked as an armaments officer. He later served as a squadron adjutant, during which time he was responsible for personnel matters, reports, payroll and other paperwork. "Once a month I signed for what seemed at the time a large amount of cash and handed it out to trainees going through the payroll line."[67]

The couple's first son, Gene Clayton, was born on October 8, 1951, at Fitzsimmons Army Hospital in Denver. While Jo was in the delivery room, she listened to the radio broadcast of Game 4 of the New York Yankees/New York Giants World Series, while the nascent father paced the waiting room. It's not known whether she listened as the Giants finished the game that day with a 6–2 win over the Yankees. And while much of the country cheered or lamented the Yankees' series win in six games, it's unlikely the new parents paid much attention.[68]

Although peace talks between North and South Korea, which began on February 1, 1951, would stall for several more years, it was becoming clear that the conflict was winding down. Officers, like Blackledge, who were on indefinite appointments, could request immediate discharge—an option Blackledge took without hesitation:

I would get less pay and more trouble as a newspaper guy than I would by staying in the Air Force. But I was ready and eager to give the civilian working world a try. Years later as I watched career military guys retiring in their 30s and 40s and starting new careers, I wondered if I had made a mistake. I think with my previous tour in the Army, beginning as a reservist at 17, I probably could have started drawing military retirement pay at 37. That would have been nice. But I never really regretted the decision to get out.[69]

When the job Blackledge had applied for after seeing an ad in *Editor & Publisher* came through in the spring of 1952, the young family headed for Russell, Kansas, some 365 miles east of Denver. Blackledge had snared his first dream job: editor of the small *Russell Daily News*. By the time the Blackledges came to town, the oil boom that lasted through the 1930s was long over in Russell County. Still, the town of some six thousand citizens managed to support two daily newspapers located right across the street from each other. Blackledge thought at the time that the situation was overkill, as indeed it proved to be. Throughout the years, several area newspapers—including the *Russell Daily News*—merged to become the *Russell County News*, the last remaining local newspaper, now published weekly on Thursdays.

As it turned out, Blackledge's title of editor had been considerably overstated. Although the editor did some editing, the job also entailed wire story selection, front-page layout, sports coverage, photography, darkroom technician work and handling local news that was phoned or dropped in personally. The newspaper's publisher, Russ Townsley, covered the traditional news beats, including the courthouse, sheriff's office and city hall. Twice weekly, Blackledge drove out of town to pick up handwritten country correspondence from stringers—the first trip was thirty miles to the east and the second thirty miles to the west of Russell. "Luckily, I didn't have to retype it," Blackledge recalled.[70] That job fell to the newspaper's lone Linotype operator. The rest of the staff included the woman who handled society news and the other owner, Al Evans, advertising manager.

One of the town's two most famous citizens was Robert Dole, the then up-and-coming Republican politician,[71] whom Blackledge said he never got to interview. "That was one of the areas Russ Townsley covered," he commented.[72] The other famous Russell resident was Arlen Specter, the Democrat, then Republican, then Democrat U.S. senator for Pennsylvania for thirty years. But by the time Blackledge got to town, the Specter family had moved to Philadelphia.[73]

At the time Blackledge interviewed for the Russell, Kansas position, the paper's owners had warned the young man that housing was in short supply, but eager to fill the spot, they offered to help secure a place for the young family. The second-floor apartment the Blackledges moved into was dingy and small, requiring that furniture be put in storage. Then, less than five months on the job, the new editor learned that his predecessor was getting out of the army earlier than expected and wanted his job back. "He's welcome to it," Blackledge said.[74] And despite the offer of a position as sports editor at another Townsley newspaper, the *Great Bend (KS) Tribune*, Blackledge opted to join the news staff of the *North Platte Daily Telegraph-Bulletin*. Blackledge said he didn't want to get typecast as a sports editor. He also wanted to get out of western Kansas—and away from any Townsley newspaper—even more. But in retrospect, Blackledge said that his experience at the *Daily News* was one of the best things that could have happened to him. He learned quickly how to work in a darkroom, as well as to write and edit without wasting time. Blackledge recalled another lesson that his first professional newspaper experience taught him:

> One day the paper was so tight there was no room for the obituaries on the inside. They would have to go on my precious page 1. I balked. "This isn't the Kansas City Star, you know," Al Evans argued. The ridiculousness of that comparison stunned me. The obits went on the front page, and I still had my self-respect the next day. It was a lesson that stayed with me.[75]

In the fall of 1952, Blackledge arrived in North Platte, Nebraska, to begin a job as a reporter at the *Telegraph-Bulletin*. When the paper's newest hire rolled into town, Mayor Kirk Mendenhall[76] had been in office a little more than a year and was already making good on his campaign promise to eliminate wide-open gambling and prostitution in North Platte. The newspaper Blackledge was joining had supported the mayor and the reform movement that eventually would bring to an end to decades of commercial vice and government corruption in North Platte, dubbed the "Little Chicago of the West." Under Mendenhall's new police chief, Charles Dick, the "rooming houses" all would eventually close.

One can only speculate as to what Blackledge knew of the town's history or its native son William M. "Bill" Jeffers in 1952.[77] When Jeffers died within the cub reporter's first year at the newspaper, it is likely that Blackledge quickly learned about Jeffers's importance to the city and the many landmarks that bore his name. For example, Jeffers Viaduct had opened to carry traffic over the Union Pacific Railroad in 1937, the same year Jeffers became president of the Union Pacific Railroad. Other namesakes included Jeffers Street, Jeffers Pavilion and Jeffers Field. In 2007, the Lincoln County Historical Society nominated Jeffers to the Nebraska Hall of Fame. Blackledge had called for and boosted his nomination in a number of his "Your Town and Mine" columns. Jeffers, however, would lose to botanist Charles Edwin Bessey, chancellor of the University of Nebraska.

In 1952, North Platte, the Lincoln County seat, was the state's fifth-largest city in size. The town's population was nearly 15,500, having experienced a hefty 26 percent increase from 1940 to 1950, due in large part to wartime rail traffic. Situated between the North and South Platte Rivers, the town was served by Highway 30 east and west and by Highway 83 north and south. Highway 30, then a major tourist and through route across the state, often was congested with traffic and home to some serious road crashes, especially during the summer months.

As Blackledge drove the nearly four-hour stretch north from Russell to North Platte that spring, it's possible that he turned the dial from one local AM radio station to the other in search of music and news. Perhaps he heard Kay Starr belt out "Wheel of Fortune," the number-one popular song at the time. Or he might have listened to the news updates as eastern Nebraska continued to reel from mid-April's devastating Missouri River flood.[78] Maybe his thoughts turned to the polio epidemic, which looked to be worsening, or to Wisconsin senator Joseph McCarthy's seemingly endless probe to expose communists in high places.

During his first year as a reporter, whenever Blackledge drove through the eastern outskirts of town on Highway 30, he passed a mile or so of cabin camps and small businesses. On the western edge, he certainly noticed that North Platte was rapidly building up with motels and filling stations interspersed with numerous residences, a drive-in theater and the fairgrounds.[79] Impressive, too, was the physical presence of the Union Pacific Railroad. In addition to UP's shops, freight yards, offices and an immense icing plant, one of the largest train classification yards in the country was located just west of town.[80]

Decades later, Blackledge remembered his first impression of North Platte:

> So as the second half of the 20th century began, North Platte had the feel of a town where anything might be possible. There was also a strong sense of opportunity for citizen participation not dominated by an entrenched establishment.[81]

Indeed, the town's railroad history frequently provided the topic for many of Blackledge's "Your Town and Mine" columns throughout the years:

> *We were born with the construction of the Union Pacific through this stretch of prairie in 1866....In 1968 the UP built a second yard, making this at the time the largest and most modern facility of its kind in the country. In 1971, the UP added a diesel repair shop. In 1978, more than 1,700 railroad men and women worked in North Platte, many of them for excellent wages.*[82]

The first newspaper in North Platte, the *Frontier Index*, was established in the fall of 1866 by Legh Freeman.[83] The paper, also called the press on wheels, was published in a boxcar for the scant citizenry residing mostly in sod houses and a few frame dwellings. It's unclear how long the *Frontier Index* lasted in North Platte, but it was likely brief because Freeman never stayed in one place too long, moving from one railroad town to the next and taking the press on wheels with him.[84]

Like most country towns of the time, North Platte was served by many, though short-lived, newspapers, including the *North Platte Daily Record*, the *Saturday Record*, the *North Platte Democrat*, the *North Platte Semi Weekly Tribune* and the *North Platte Republican*.[85] The *North Platte Daily Telegraph* and the *North Platte Daily Bulletin* both enjoyed separate and enduring histories. These two publications, which merged in 1946, formed the *Telegraph-Bulletin*, the paper Blackledge was joining in 1952.

The *Telegraph* was founded on April 14, 1881, as an afternoon newspaper. Subscription price: two dollars per year. "The front page was two columns of mostly advertising and five columns passed off as news."[86] Although the *Telegraph* missed by nearly a decade the opportunity to report on the arrival by train in North Platte of Grand Duke Alexis of Russia for a buffalo hunt guided by William F. Cody,[87] on January 13, 1872, the newspaper was there to inform readers about President Theodore Roosevelt's car stop in May 1905. The opening of the Keith Theater in 1908, the dedication of the new Carnegie Library in 1912 and the showing of *The Jazz Singer*, the country's first all-talking movie during the 1928 holiday season, all made the news. The paper described the "massive brick building, two stories in height" in 1917 to report construction of the town's fire station and city offices on Front Street. And when the Fox Theater opened on November 24, 1922, the *Telegraph* headline proclaimed it to be "Wonder House Best in the West." There were bad news stories too. For example, the paper told readers about the destruction by fire of the Lincoln County Courthouse on April 30, 1923, as well as the later news that the blaze had been set by County Treasurer Samuel Souder in an effort to conceal embezzlement of county funds. The final story about the sad set of events was Souder's conviction of arson on December 23, 1923.[88]

The *Daily Bulletin* began as a four-page tabloid shopping guide on April 13, 1932. Throughout the 1930s and 1940s, both the *Bulletin* and the *Telegraph* served North Platte and Lincoln County. The *Bulletin* and *Telegraph* were published in the mornings and afternoons, respectively. When Joe W. Seacrest of Lincoln purchased the two newspapers in 1946 to establish the *Telegraph-Bulletin*, the morning publishing schedule was abandoned. On April 17, 2003—fifty-seven years after the merger—the *Bulletin* was revived as a weekly, making North Platte unique as a two-newspaper city.[89]

When Blackledge first arrived on the job, the *Telegraph-Bulletin* office was located on East Fifth Street. The newsroom was on the first floor:

> *It was smack up against the plate glass windows where any passerby could see whether the news staff and the editor were working or not.... The main disadvantage of the first-floor location was the terrible accessibility. Anyone could bolt in off the street and come face to face with the editor without an instant's notice. Not a thoroughly happy situation. Frequent questions. Why did you say this? Why didn't you do this? Editors do not always know. What effect this had on editors of those days we cannot say for certain. One quit and went to work for the licensed beverage industry. Another became such an accomplished talker that he took up law and is now on his way to becoming a wealthier man than any editor of our acquaintance.*[90]

The newsroom later would move to the second floor and then back again to the first floor before the entire operation relocated in 1981 to its current Chestnut Street address. As Blackledge recalled:

> *The newspaper was a grimy place, filled with the smell of molten lead and the clatter of linotype machines. Reporters typed their stories on ancient battered typewriters. News copy was typed usually on sheets of newsprint cut from pressroom waste. It went to a copy editor, who marked it up with heavy black pencil and sent on to a typesetter, who worked at a large machine with a strange keyboard that translated the copy into lines of type cast from molten lead. A reporter didn't have to be a neat typist, just fast.*[91]

Blackledge said that the newsroom typewriters were essentially one step away from being antiques—or junk:

> *But no matter how old and battered that big old, black, standard typewriter was, you got used to its "feel" and were most comfortable writing at that typewriter in preference to any other. When a writer is comfortable, the words flow more easily. Sometimes.*[92]

When Blackledge joined the *Telegraph-Bulletin*'s news staff in 1952, C.H. George Cooper was the general manager. Blackledge referred to him as "Gentle George." But things were in disarray in the news department under the managing editor at the time. "We were drifting. I wasn't getting many, if any, story assignments. It worried me. I had a wife and son to support, I needed a job, and I didn't want to move again for a while."[93] So the cub reporter asked the sports editor and advertising manager Jim Kirkman if he could use some assistance.[94] Indeed he could. Blackledge began writing sports, and within a short time, when Kirkman wanted to step aside as sports editor to concentrate on advertising, Blackledge became the *Telegraph-Bulletin*'s new sports editor. "So there you go," Blackledge quipped. "Turn down a sports job because you didn't want to be typed or trapped in it. End up taking another sports job."[95]

Blackledge covered high school football, basketball and track. Then, to his dismay, he learned that the sports editor also was expected to be the official scorer for Nebraska's Independent League games, the semi-professional baseball team that played at Jeffers ballpark. Blackledge referred to Joe di Natale of radio station KODY as his savior.[96] While Di Natale announced the games, Blackledge sat by his side:

> *Di Natale would give me a not-subtle clue as to whether the play was a hit or an error, and announce without necessarily waiting for my response, "the official scorer has ruled…" I was forever grateful. Gradually I began to understand and enjoy the game.*[97]

Then there was the mishap in the summer of 1952 that sent Blackledge to the hospital. While on vacation, Blackledge figured that he'd take the opportunity to photograph events at the National High School Rodeo at Harrison, Nebraska. Blackledge snapped the shot as the state's all-around high school cowboy champ was tying a calf—just moments before the boy's saddle bronc trampled the young photographer, sending him to the Lusk, Wyoming hospital for treatment of his injuries.

Meanwhile, Blackledge grabbed any straight news opportunities he could to prove himself busy and productive. Soon he and Kirkman began sharing the former sports editor's "Dots and Dashes" weekly sports column. Blackledge was particularly proud of the column he wrote titled "In Memorial," which was reprinted in the program for the North Platte–Lexington football game. In the piece, Blackledge paid tribute to North Platte High School football athletes Jerry Wellman, Dick Anderson and Arlon Keeten, along with businessman and sports fan Beeler Scott, who piloted the plane that crashed on October 31, 1953, killing them all. The group had been en route to a University of Nebraska football game in Lincoln when the plane crashed into a fog-shrouded hill near Brady.

Blackledge once commented that North Platte was a town where news happened. For example, within several months of his arrival at the paper, North Platte's own Robert B. Crosby was elected governor of Nebraska. On October 28, 1953, King Paul and Queen Frederica of Greece passed through North Platte during their tour of the United States, as Blackledge reported in the article headlined "Queen Has Early Appetite: Scribe Shown Menu Instead of Royalty This Morning."

One year later, when the movie *The Glenn Miller Story* came to the North Platte's Fox Theater, readers may have been surprised to learn that the "Jazz King Was a Youngster Here," as the headline avowed. According to the article, the movie was proof that "North Platte is a good place as any to start on the road to fame." The famous musician lived with his parents in North Platte until he was thirteen, when the family left for Grant City, Oklahoma.[98]

Finally determined to improve the newspaper, General Manager Cooper called the inept managing editor into his office and gave him a copy of *Editor & Publisher* turned to the help wanted pages. Cooper named another managing editor, hired a new sports editor and moved Blackledge into straight news reporting:

> *We started early, worked hard and fast, and when the paper came off the presses in early afternoon, our time was more or less our own. There were things to be done for the next day's paper, and night meetings or games to cover, and calls on the fatal accidents that old Highway 30 traffic produced with grim regularity. But on many afternoons, Harry and I could slip out early for fishing or hunting. Even at that, we probably put in 60 hours or so most weeks, with no suggestion of overtime. But we soaked up lots of newspaper experience in a few years and had great fun doing it.[99]*

Left: Fishing buddies Harry Contos (*left*) and Blackledge. Both were reporters at the *North Platte Telegraph-Bulletin* in the early 1950s. *Blackledge Collection.*

Below: Keith Blackledge with one of the many awards he would receive throughout his lifetime. *Blackledge Collection.*

The "Harry" Blackledge was referring to was Harry Contos, who covered the police, the sheriff's office and the courts. Contos eventually was promoted to managing editor.[100] Blackledge became city editor and took over most of the top beats that had been his predecessor's territory. When Contos left the newspaper in 1956 to go to law school, Blackledge became the new managing editor. "I got his job but lost a hunting and fishing partner."[101]

Soon Blackledge began writing opinion columns for the paper's editorial page. The date of the earliest "Letter from the Editor: Your Town and Mine" found among his papers is September 9, 1957. The column, which was published periodically from 1957 to 1959, consisted mostly of the writer's musings on a variety of topics.

In the meantime, Blackledge was getting noticed outside the *Telegraph-Bulletin* office. On September 2, 1959, the Nebraska Jaycees named Blackledge Nebraska Outstanding Young Man at the state convention. He'd been selected North Platte's Jaycees' Outstanding Young Man earlier that year.

Also, in the intervening years, the Blackledge family had grown to five with the births of Mark Allen, the couple's middle son, on May 14, 1953, and their youngest, Victor Roy, on May 22, 1956.

But as the decade was coming to a close, Blackledge was ready to give big-city journalism a try. In December, 1959, the thirty-three-year-old Blackledge resigned his position as managing editor of the *Telegraph-Bulletin* to join the news staff of the *Miami (FL) Herald*.

Chapter 3

BIG-CITY JOURNALISM

I began in this business with the idea that putting words on paper could be interesting work, and if you did it well, those words might help people understand better the community and the world we all share. The world seems to have gotten harder to explain. But the fundamentals haven't changed greatly. Get it right, to the best of your knowledge at the moment. Know you will make mistakes, and correct them quickly. Be fair. Be honest. Check the spelling. Don't use big words if little words will do. Don't take yourself too seriously.
—Keith Blackledge[102]

Keith, Jo and their three young sons headed to Florida early in 1960. While the lion's share of Miami's new arrivals stayed there—large-scale migration to the state's southernmost city had begun following Cuba's 1959 revolution—the Blackledges would live and work some thirty miles north in Fort Lauderdale, another Florida city that had experienced a massive postwar population explosion. Blackledge was joining the *Miami Herald* as the Fort Lauderdale bureau chief.

How different the Florida surroundings must have seemed to the midwesterners. Instead of flat plains and prairie, there were palm trees and ocean beaches. From cold and dreary to warm and sunny. From small town to metropolitan. North Platte, the town they'd called home for the past seven years, had a population of some 17,000 in 1960, while Miami's population that year was 291,700 and Fort Lauderdale had grown to nearly 83,650.

Blackledge was going to work for a very different kind of newspaper. The *Miami Herald*, established in 1910, gained a reputation early on for hard-hitting journalism and outstanding local coverage. Nine years prior to Blackledge's arrival, the *Herald* had earned its first Pulitzer Prize for Public Service for its exposé of government corruption in southern Florida. The publisher, John S. Knight, who bought the paper in 1937, would eventually build the Knight Ridder newspaper chain, one of the country's largest. The year Blackledge arrived, Knight constructed a $30 million facility containing the newspaper's offices and printing presses. It was the biggest building in Florida and the most extensive newspaper printing plant of the time.

Letters Blackledge wrote to family and friends provide glimpses of life and work in Florida. In his first letter to friend Ted Turpin,[103] who succeeded him as managing editor of the *North Platte Telegraph-Bulletin*, Blackledge described his position as the Fort Lauderdale bureau chief:

> *I'm enjoying my job. But it's a strange experience. I feel sometimes like a guy groping through a closet full of clothes, unable to find the door or the light. So many deadlines to watch I can't keep track of them, and such a balancing act to conduct—get a good story, does the* News [Fort Lauderdale's competing daily newspaper] *have it too? Do we have to run it now or could we save it for Thursday or Sunday? If we save it will the* News *beat us to it? Or should we maybe do it all over with a different approach? Can we get the makeup man to give it proper position and play? I used to think how nice it would be to have a full eight-hour day to put in on one day's paper. But there is never any release from the deadlines either. Every time you finish one job, you know there are three or four things you ought to be seeing about. Then, I leave most evenings at 6, 7 or 8 with some stories yet to come in, and final deadline still four to two hours away so something might yet happen. When I get up in the morning I have to rush out to the doorstep to find out what sort of product was produced the day before.*[104]

With that, Blackledge's letter came to an abrupt close. "Just had a call from Miami. Plane crash in Indiana. Fort Lauderdale woman aboard; we can pick up picture and drive it in to get in under deadline…maybe. Will finish this another time. klb."

An additional challenge for Blackledge was managing the news team—a first for the untried bureau chief. "Have some really good people on my little staff but there are personnel problems here too," Blackledge told Turpin, lamenting the fact that one reporter was transferred to the Miami shop while another had quit the bureau to take a job in Oregon. Still, Blackledge was optimistic. "I've got a really great little gal with some personality problems to overcome, and a good reporter from Miami filling the gaps temporarily with two new hands scheduled to start first of April," he said.[105]

But by late summer, Blackledge's staff problems seemed to have worsened. "Everybody in Florida is crazy, except maybe me, and I'm not so sure any longer about me," he wrote. "Two of my staffers are seeing a psychiatrist regularly and several others should be. Everybody is always unhappy about something. There is a steady diet of gossip and rumor through the entire *Herald* staff."[106] Blackledge then went on to characterize the Fort Lauderdale news team. There was Mike, "a wordy obtuse lazy prima donna who nevertheless has considerable talent." Blackledge described George as "a good reporter, imaginative writer, aggressive and hardworking, but he doesn't like living where people live in houses and mow lawns. He longs for apartment buildings of New York." He called the reporter named Gail "a 24-year-old baby who has unlimited ability but is really almost to the point of being a dangerous psychotic." And in Bev he saw "a great news gal who is beginning to realize, at 33, that the job isn't enough to keep you from being lonely."[107] In sum, Blackledge wrote:

There are others who are more or less sane, more or less interesting. A couple with good potential and some with none at all. But at any rate it seems to me some times that all have troubles, and I should have majored in psychiatry rather than journalism.[108]

Within months of Blackledge's arrival at the *Herald*, the threat of a strike among pressmen, stereotypers and mailers loomed over the newspaper, but publisher Knight was prepared. Anticipating a walkout, managers were trained in the operation of the printing press. Housed in the so-called newspaper annex halfway across the city, the *Herald* maintained a secondary press used to print special sections and extra copies of the Sunday edition. There the *Herald*'s administrators shed sport coats, loosened ties and rolled up sleeves to produce four eight-page sections involving several practice runs on the six-unit Goss Headliner press, with four color half-decks and two folders. Blackledge described the training:

We got a lecture, then actual practice in pasting up, webbing up, plating up, running the press and adjusting for margin, etcetera. By the end of the week we were running full color, registering it, and doing a pretty fair job....As one guy said late one afternoon when we were all hot, sweaty, inky, greasy and tired, "Now I know why pressmen are all so mean. I really feel that way myself."[109]

Blackledge didn't say if the unions went out on strike at the time; however, people far and near came to "the only place in the country where there is a fully operational, metropolitan size newspaper press available simply for practice and instruction."[110]

That winter, the Florida Associated Press held its meeting in Fort Lauderdale, giving Blackledge the opportunity to attend a workshop on newspaper makeup led by a University of Florida professor. To Blackledge, the information about newspaper design was fascinating:

I sat there and ached to try all these ideas in the Telegraph-Bulletin. *The* Herald *already uses most of them. The "trend" seems to be to do lots of horizontal makeup, lots of "boxing off" stories under multiple column heads....Makeup of inside pages was particularly emphasized. There really are some great things that can be done if you just can take the time and effort.*[111]

Blackledge went on to provide tips to his *Telegraph-Bulletin* successor, explaining how white space can be used effectively and how horizontal page design can be accomplished by spreading stories seven columns across eight columns on the page. Blackledge said he learned that nearly all the Florida dailies were "ahead of the trend" in modern makeup techniques.[112]

One day, when Blackledge was in the Miami offices, he met Rae Weimer, the journalism director at the University of Florida, who was in town for a convention. The two struck up a conversation and soon discovered a connection to North Platte, Nebraska. Turns out, Weimer and his brother, Claud, owned and operated the *North Platte Herald* from 1925 to 1926.[113] However, the Weimers quickly learned not only that the former owner had misrepresented the circulation numbers but also that he had sold them a load of bills along with the paper. After struggling for about a year, the Weimers said that they finally paid off the one good female employee they had, closed the doors and left town. The brothers stopped in York, Nebraska, thinking to get jobs, but when they saw the headline in the York newspaper declaring that the Weimer brothers had skipped North Platte, they just kept going. "My brother and I got out of town one jump ahead of the sheriff and the bill collectors," Blackledge quoted Weimer in a letter to Turpin.[114]

That fall, Blackledge wrote to friends about a *Miami Herald* press party he'd attended for the cast of *Where the Boys Are*, a coming-of-age film about four midwestern college girls on spring break in Fort Lauderdale. Blackledge described the party participants as "movie type people," without mentioning any of the stars he might have met: Connie Francis, Paula Prentiss, Dolores Hart, Yvette Mimieux, George Hamilton or Jim Hutton. What clearly was of more interest to Blackledge was the time he was spending in the Miami newsroom that fall filling in for a vacationing editorial writer:

> *First day Don Shoemaker* [editorial page editor] *suggested I do an editorial on the election in Brazil. What election? In 30 minutes with the help of* The New York Times *and the* Encyclopedia Britannica *I was an expert. Some fun. Then he told me he would be gone this Thursday and Friday and I would be in charge. Who, me? In charge of the editorial page of the great* Miami Herald? *Gawsh.*[115]

Management apparently liked Blackledge's commentaries, for he later spent three weeks in what was called the *Miami Herald*'s Ivory Tower, where the writers pounded out their editorials. According to Blackledge:

> *It is enjoyable. So quiet and unhurried....I have come to grips editorially with elections in Brazil and South Africa; the closing of a consulate in Panama; and President Eisenhower's birthday. Nothing on Afghanistan yet, but I'm working up to the really big stuff.*[116]

The substitute editorial writer drove the hour-and-fifteen-minute commute each day from Fort Lauderdale to Miami. And while he disliked what he called the daily fender battle, he liked the job. "I think if I got an offer to be an editorial writer on a fulltime basis I would be tempted. So comfortable. So relaxed. So intellectual."[117]

Blackledge was not offered a permanent assignment as an editorial writer, but on November 11, 1960, he became an assistant city editor of the *Herald*—a position he reluctantly accepted. Blackledge figured that he needed the job in order to move up within the newsroom hierarchy. By that time, his interest had narrowed to a few select slots, one of which was a chief editorial writing position he'd been told was in the works. If nothing to his liking came through within a year or so, he would leave the *Herald*. For the time being, however, he pledged to learn all he could before abandoning the venture.

In letters to friend Turpin following his promotion, Blackledge made several references to turmoil at the paper:

All hell has been breaking on the Herald.... *The* Fun in Florida *editor quit in a huff with the new director of graphic arts. A city editor from Charlotte had marital troubles and moved down here, though what that had to do with settling them I don't know. How I fit into all of this I don't know either.*[118]

But fit in he eventually did. As he told Turpin:

Am beginning to catch on now a little and feel a little more sure of myself. It is damn hard being in a position where you are theoretically supposed to be directing people and don't know the first thing about what is going on while they know a good deal. They are very particular about makeup here, and particular that it is done their way but not quite sure what their way is until they see it done "wrong" and then they will tell you.... I was pretty miserable.[119]

In March, Blackledge participated in the American Press Institute for managing editors and publishers from throughout the country at Columbia University in New York City. While there, he and several other seminar participants attended the theater performance of *My Fair Lady*, which was celebrating its fifth anniversary on Broadway that year. While reading the program, Blackledge noticed the name Loren Driscoll, the American tenor, playing the part of Freddy Eynsford-Hill. Driscoll and Blackledge were in the same Boy Scout patrol as kids in Scottsbluff, and Driscoll sang at the Blackledges' wedding. The theater usher delivered a note from the newspaperman to the performer, who invited the group backstage after the show. Blackledge said that it was hard not to notice how impressed the other newspaper executives were with the small-town guy from Nebraska and his connection to the star.[120]

As one of the *Herald*'s five assistant city editors, Blackledge mostly worked the shift from 4:00 p.m. to 1:00 a.m. and some weekends. Two editors were on each shift, with the so-called slot man directing the actual operation of the city staff, including making assignments, while the second editor occupied himself solely with designing the local page. Blackledge explained that the local page was either the front of the B or C sections to showcase the best local news:

I realized at one point that the trouble may be this is the first newspaper job I ever had where you had time to think. It is considerably less worrisome just doing things quickly and excusing your mistakes on the grounds you were fighting a deadline then it is sitting down at 7 p.m. with nothing to do but make a page by 11 p.m.—but with the responsibility of making sure it is right, clever, imaginative.[121]

Some shifts, though, would be different. Blackledge worked ten days straight during the second and third weeks in April 1961, during which time foreign correspondents flocked to the *Herald* newsroom desperate for information about America's invasion of the Bay of Pigs on the south coast of Cuba. The journalists started arriving even before the first failed airstrike to bomb Cuban airfields occurred on April 15. Over the next several days, events continued to unfold in Cuba, with Fidel Castro ultimately succeeding at crushing the botched incursion on April 19. In the meantime, international journalists packed the newsroom:

From English, Canadian, Australian newspapers—even one guy hanging around the office several days from a Japanese newspaper and making calls on our phones to Tokyo (collect, I trust). They mostly hung around and read the wire stories over each other's shoulders, taking notes and I assume rewriting them as exclusive dispatches. World's most frustrating story—nobody could find out anything or find any way to get anywhere they might find out something. Thousands of words moved daily and not a fact among them.[122]

Blackledge took two full days off following what he called the "Cuban war" to do nothing but fish. Then, on May 1, 1961, Blackledge caught another unusual shift. "Talk about news," he said:

Monday night we were on pins and needles waiting for word—expected by midnight—on whether the astronaut shoot was going off or not. Our front page was pretty well committed to that as the lead—with a six-column artist's drawing of the path of the rocket, etcetera. Then at about 5 we heard a National Airlines plane was missing between Marathon and Key West. A couple of hours later that finally turned up in Cuba—had been hijacked. And before the evening was over it had flown back to Key West, and then the pilot and crew were flown back here—a hot running story with changing developments every five minutes and one that would have been a great lead story if it hadn't been for the space shoot. Along the way, small

*minor annoyances—a hit and run traffic fatality, a body found floating in
a lake, a suicide—popped up during the evening. Then they didn't shoot the
darn astronaut. Disgusting.*[123]

The astronaut was Alan B. Shepard Jr., who in his Freedom 7 Mercury
capsule successfully lifted off from Cape Canaveral on May 5, 1961, to
become the first American to fly into space. The plane hijacking of National
Airlines Flight 337, bound for Key West from Miami, ended without physical
injuries after the pilot flew the hijacker, a thirty-five-year-old Puerto Rican,
to Havana, and the plane returned to Florida.

A few days later, Blackledge dragged his typewriter outside to his backyard
patio to write letters:

*I feel almost guilty right now. Beautiful day. Must be about 78 degrees, a
gentle breeze rustling the banana tree and giving a little movement to some
sort of deep purple-red flowers hanging over the back fence. Sky is Florida-
blue with a few light, white clouds. A blue jay just flew by, and a cardinal
is due any minute. A squirrel ran across the telephone wire from our mango
tree to the neighbor's a few minutes ago. Delightful.*[124]

But Blackledge's letters also revealed glimmers of discontent:

*The job is, except occasionally, rather unsatisfying. It doesn't seem at the
end of the day like you've done much on most days. But it is impossible to
describe and impossible to understand until you are into it, how complex it
is turning out a big multi-edition paper. This complexity makes this ultra-
division of labor necessary, I guess, and carries with it a lot of confusion
and seeming inefficiency that is just inevitable.*[125]

He continued to describe the situation. The local man, who makes up the
local page, doesn't write his own headlines, but rather decides what headline
he wants and then passes the story to the copy desk, where the head is written
and passed back to the local man for approval. The recently hired picture
editor on the city desk makes photo assignments, crops pictures, occasionally
writes cutlines and keeps track of the photographers—all duties that had
formerly been handled by assistant city editors:

*Naturally it is hard sometimes to know whether you are supposed to be
doing something or someone else is. Sometimes reporters find themselves*

*getting assignments from two editors who have forgotten to coordinate....
This is the newspaper business?*[126]

In the spring of 1961, the Blackledges, planning a three-week vacation to Nebraska, plopped down $1,595 to purchase a white 1959 Rambler station wagon, with factory air conditioning, to drive the trip. The vacation that July and August included time in Scottsbluff with the couple's parents and then on to North Platte for visits with friends. At the trip's end, the Blackledges knew that they wouldn't return to Miami. In his letters from Florida, which span from March 1960 until May 30, 1961, Blackledge occasionally commented on the financial hard times that had befallen the *Herald*, the economic slump in Miami and Fort Lauderdale and the massive influx of Cubans who found no work. That summer, two events grabbed the headlines. A series of demonstrations and wade-ins began in July at Miami's public beaches to protest the city's policy of racial segregation. In August, the Miami Newspaper Pressmen's Local No. 46 began picketing, although the *Herald* was able to continue publishing.[127]

After accepting an offer to teach at the University of Nebraska's School of Journalism, Blackledge returned to Miami to put in his two weeks' notice. That fall, the Blackledges were back in Nebraska, where the newspaperman took graduate classes in history and taught beginning reporting and photography. He worked Saturday nights on the copy desk at the *Lincoln Journal*. Three years later, however, Blackledge was tired of teaching. "I couldn't stand my own lectures, and I needed more money," he later told an interviewer.[128]

Then the page-one story in the June 15, 1964 edition of the *Dayton Journal Herald* announced the appointment of Keith Blackledge, age thirty-seven, to the news staff.

The family, their fully loaded Rambler pointed nearly straight east, left Lincoln that summer to make the 760-mile trip on Highway 36 to Dayton, Ohio. With the station wagon's air conditioner blasting, the boys relieved their boredom during the near twelve-hour trip by competing for points as they counted the vehicles with license plates from as many states as possible (although there were few besides Nebraska, Kansas and eventually Illinois, Indiana and Ohio). When the competition became too fierce, attempts were made to locate a static-free AM station that broadcast something besides country-western music or farm reports. The boys—now eight, eleven and nearly thirteen—wanted the Beatles. So, instead of the radio, their sweet young voices joined in song. "I Want to Hold Your Hand" was the favorite during that journey to Dayton. However, in August, the Animals' "House of the Rising Sun" was released in the United States, and it would become the family's number-one a cappella choice during future excursions for years to come. When Job, Peter & Chuck, a North Platte music ensemble, performed the song during Blackledge's funeral service on July 8, 2010, there wasn't a dry eye in the sanctuary.

Blackledge, who was joining the *Journal Herald* staff of five editorial writers, missed getting to know Erma Bombeck, who a decade earlier had written for the newspaper from her home and was paid a modest amount per column.[129] By the time Blackledge was on board, the nationally syndicated humor columnist's "At Wit" was published in hundreds of newspapers throughout the nation.

Blackledge hadn't been on the job for a week when he'd been told by more than one person on the news staff about the May 5, 1863 fire that destroyed the *Journal* building—the stuff of newspaper legends. As the story went, the newspaper had so irritated supporters of proslavery "peace Democrat" Clement Vallandigham that they formed a mob, cut all the telegraph wires and torched the building.[130]

The *Journal Herald* was founded by publisher of the *Dayton Daily News*, James M. Cox, who purchased and combined the two morning newspapers in 1949.[131] The idea was to pioneer a kind of journalism based on objectivity and public advocacy while avoiding ties to advertisers and politicians. Nonetheless, the *Journal Herald* clearly held to its Republican traditions, while the *Daily News* was ideologically Democrat. Both Cox newspapers were produced in the same building in downtown Dayton. The two newsrooms were on separate floors, while the publications shared the same press. According to Blackledge, "They preserved a fierce news-side competition and a vigorous difference in editorial points of view."[132] When the *Journal Herald* and the *Daily News* merged in 1986, Blackledge explained to readers the imprecision of the terms "liberal" and "conservative," which often were used to compare the two papers:

> *The* Journal Herald *of my memory had been as progressive, independent and provocative as a newspaper can be. It acknowledged a Republican history, but its editorial position on any issue could not have been predicted by any label, either of politics or ideology.... The* Journal Herald *refused to endorse Barry Goldwater. And since it could not bring itself to endorse a Democrat and thus be on the same side as the* Daily News, *it was left hanging on the fence in that presidential election. But its real strength was in the sharp and courageous views it brought to local issues.*[133]

Although Blackledge said that he never missed his time at the *Journal Herald*, he respected its crusty editor, Glenn Thompson, a Princeton graduate who came to the paper in 1959. As Blackledge described him:

> *Thompson came from a Southern Democratic background. He was conservative on some issues, liberal on others, but mostly unpredictable and independent on every issue. He thought well and cared deeply and believed that a newspaper's duty was to speak for what was right, not for what was ideologically or politically appropriate.*[134]

Thompson also liked short editorials, and Blackledge could whip them out pretty quickly, sometimes writing four or five a day. In addition to brevity, Blackledge learned that an effective editorialist doesn't get stuck on one subject or theme. Another lasting impression was Thompson's support of arts and culture, especially in hick towns, as he referred to them. Thompson thought that Dayton was a hick town because it wasn't New York City, and he told Blackledge that a good newspaper editor should champion education and the arts, especially in small communities.[135] Such were the teachings from Dayton, Ohio, and Blackledge practiced them throughout his long newspaper career.

After the two newspapers combined to become the *Dayton Daily News–Journal Herald* in 1986, Blackledge cracked, "You would not expect a mouthful like that to last beyond the next redesign of the front page."[136]

When the Blackledges arrived in Dayton in 1964, the city had twice the population of Lincoln. But the summers in both places were the same: hot and sticky. Dayton, population roughly 262,000 in 1964, was the sixth-largest city in Ohio.

That same summer, a major construction project had begun to extend Sixth Street through to Wilkinson Street to accommodate increased automobile traffic to downtown Dayton. With the majestic Union Station at Sixth and Ludlow blocking the street, crews had already started demolition of the station and its seven-story clock tower. Built in 1901, the station was often described as a handsome palace where thousands of travelers had congregated throughout the heydays of passenger rail service. The clock had stopped working in the late 1950s, and by the early 1960s, Dayton's passenger train needs had diminished. The razing of Dayton's Union Station was an irony that would not be lost on Blackledge many years later in North Platte, where in the early 1970s he tirelessly—and unsuccessfully—campaigned to save the old Union Pacific depot from demolition.

Eventually, Blackledge was promoted to city editor and then to assistant managing editor. He also taught an editorial writing class at Ohio State University, driving the seventy-mile jaunt from Dayton to Columbus one day a week. But after three years, Blackledge was ready to go home.

On August 31, 1967, the *Journal Herald* announced Blackledge's resignation to head the news-editorial operation at the *North Platte Telegraph*, a position he held until his retirement in 1992. And for the next twenty-five years, Blackledge wrote almost daily editorials and his weekly column, "Your Town and Mine," until his death in 2010. He said that the column's title was meant to suggest that "wherever we live, and whatever our differences, there is a shared interest in working to make the town better."[137]

Chapter 4

COMMUNITY JOURNALISM COMES TO NORTH PLATTE, NEBRASKA

That is what newspapers and their editors are supposed to do: get the problems and issues and opportunities on the table, into public discussion; offer ideas and alternatives, encourage dialogue, and support people who take an active part in seeking solutions.
—Keith Blackledge[138]

Pulitzer Prize–winning newspaper editor William Allen White of the *Emporia (KS) Gazette* blazed a journalistic trail that Keith Blackledge was determined to follow. Through his writing, which was infused with humor and a commonsense approach, White was resolute in improving his town.[139]

Blackledge was unwavering in his admiration of White, who as editor of the Kansas newspaper from 1895 to 1944 was the prototypical community journalist. According to scholars, community journalism is local; community newspapers reinforce civic engagement; and the editorial content embodies a booster philosophy that supports economic growth and social order in the towns these newspapers serve.[140]

For Blackledge, the town would be North Platte, Nebraska, and the newspaper the *North Platte Telegraph*, where in the fall of 1967 he became the paper's new executive editor. Regarding the lure to return to the *Telegraph*, he wrote:

I have lived in Los Angeles, Dayton, Fort Lauderdale, Miami, Lincoln, Denver and a few other places. I was a reporter and editor on this paper for seven years, and had a fling at larger cities, returned in 1967 to stay. North Platte is big enough to be a challenge, small enough that you sometimes feel you can make a difference.[141]

Blackledge considered White his personal hero from the time he first read his autobiography in high school. From that point on, Blackledge's destiny was set. As he later remembered:

[White's] autobiography must have shaped the dreams of hundreds of thousands of would-be journalists. I know it shaped mine....There were occasional sorties into metropolitan journalism that somehow seemed empty of purpose. Only in the small town was there the feeling that I was doing what I was meant to do. It is enough to be part of a community with the unique opportunities an editor has to share in the joys and sorrows of that community.[142]

But there was more than the pull of small-town journalism that brought Blackledge back to the *Telegraph*. For at least a year prior to his return, Blackledge had been communicating with the paper's owner, Joseph Rushton Seacrest (Joe R.), who offered the then managing editor of Dayton, Ohio's *Journal-Herald* the editorship of the *Telegraph*. Seacrest wanted a more aggressive local editorial voice. As he wrote to Blackledge:

We are not aspiring to be the most controversial newspaper for the state of Nebraska for the sake of controversy; but instead to comment in a timely manner on those controversies...and to point out and identify the problems so the community is aware of the issues and choices....Don't come if you don't like Nebraska and North Platte as a place to live; don't come if you don't intend to selectively involve yourself in some phase of North Platte life....Don't come unless you want to work hard and have a lot of self-starting zip left from the superb organization pace of larger newspapers or the academic pace of education.[143]

To sweeten the deal, Blackledge was offered exclusive control of the editorial division of the newspaper. Blackledge took the job, and the unique agreement was codified between Blackledge and the paper's owners.

Years later, Blackledge recounted the rare and privileged arrangement he'd enjoyed at the *Telegraph*:

[Joe R.] *didn't promise a rose garden, but he did promise that the editor would be able to say whatever he liked on the editorial page, free of interference or pre-judgment by owners or other administrators.... There are not many newspaper situations like that anywhere. It takes terrific discipline for an owner, officer or publisher to refrain from meddling in editorial policy.... For better or worse, I had 25 years of the kind of editorial independence usually afforded only to editors who own a newspaper. Some readers no doubt thought that was a mistake, but I will be forever grateful.*[144]

Joe R. Seacrest. *North Platte Telegraph.*

So, in the fall of 1967, Blackledge drove the thousand-mile stretch from Dayton to North Platte alone. His wife, Jo, and their three sons already were back in North Platte, preparing the house for the movers and the boys for school. Heading nearly straight west on the spanking new Interstate 80, Blackledge really didn't mind the fourteen-hour drive because it gave him plenty of time to think. His musings may have gone something like this: It was remarkable how different things were since he'd left North Platte in 1959 to take a crack at big-city journalism. Gene, now nearly sixteen, and Mark, fourteen, were teenagers, and Vic, at eleven, soon would be. Blackledge smiled remembering the trip to Dayton in 1964, when the Beatles had so captured his young sons' attention. Amazing that those four moptop musicians from Britain had lasted this long, he thought. Certainly his boys had never tired of listening to the *Sgt. Pepper's Lonely Hearts Club Band* album—over and over again—all summer long.

Blackledge had to hand it to pop musician Bob Dylan, who seemed to have gotten it right with "The Times They Are a-Changin'"—race riots in so many cities throughout the summer, and peace demonstrations increased as America's presence in Vietnam intensified. Long hair, short skirts. Glad to be returning to Nebraska.

As he drove, Blackledge's thoughts turned to the Nebraska Centennial, celebrated that year for one hundred years of statehood, and he supposed there still would be festivities going on in North Platte. He'd only recently seen the new five-cent centennial stamp featuring the image of a Hereford steer and an ear of corn. Truth be told, he preferred the image of "The

Sower" on the three-cent stamp that marked Nebraska's territorial centennial in 1954.

Too bad he'd just missed the August 27 Denver Broncos and Oakland Raiders exhibition football game. When his North Platte friend and fellow newspaperman Jim Kirkman told him that the town had snared a major professional football preseason matchup, he'd been astounded. As Blackledge heard it, the Buffalo Bills Booster Club had organized a fundraising drive to pay each team $25,000 to play in the so-called Nebraska Centennial Bowl. Tickets cost $10.25 for reserve seats and $6 for general admission. Bleachers were brought in from other communities to increase North Platte's high school stadium capacity to eleven thousand seats. And tarps were slung over the fences so people couldn't watch the game without paying. Denver, the "home team," beat Oakland, 21–17.[145]

Yes, Blackledge mused, North Platte is a place where things get done. As examples, the $12.5 million eastbound Bailey Yard hump that was nearing completion, plans that were progressing to move NEBRASKAland Days to its new home in North Platte and the openings of another bank and several new businesses. Such improvements helped to boost the town's population too, from a little over fifteen thousand in the early 1950s to more than seventeen thousand in 1960—and, he'd been told, community leaders were expecting at least nineteen thousand with the 1970 census.

But Blackledge also knew that he'd have his work cut out for him at the *Telegraph*. The newspaper business certainly was in the throes of change. In fact, he remembered, following his return to Scottsbluff, Nebraska, after the war, discussions with his dad, who back then had voiced concerns that radio was proving to be a viable source for news and was eroding newspaper readership. Advertising dollars were following suit. And since the 1950s, television! Blackledge recalled reading somewhere that the share of adult newspaper readers had declined from 85 percent in 1946 to around 70 percent in 1965. And, he feared, the downward slide could continue. And that wasn't the worst of it. With the decrease in the number of family-owned newspapers, a phenomenon that seemed to have accelerated of late, Blackledge feared that the chains were leaving behind local news. He considered himself fortunate to be joining the Seacrest operation.

The Seacrest name is synonymous with publishing in Nebraska. Joe R.'s grandfather Joseph Claggett Seacrest (J.C.) arrived in Lincoln, Nebraska, in 1867, bringing with him lots of ambition and a healthy dose of newspaper experience.[146] Since boyhood, J.C. had worked in virtually all facets of the business at his uncle's newspaper, the *Greencastle (PA) Press*. Shortly after arriving in Lincoln, he secured a position as a police reporter at one of the local papers; he later moved to the business side. Within the next ten years, J.C. would become business manager of the *Lincoln Journal*, while at the same time amassing pieces of the ownership. He wanted his newspaper to be local, the coverage fair and the writing style breezy. But most important was J.C.'s civic integrity, which well served his community service approach to journalism, a tradition he passed on to future Seacrest generations.[147]

J.C.'s sons, Joe Winger (Joe W.) and Fred, became co-publishers of the *Journal* in 1942. Joe W. had editorial control, while Fred handled production and business matters. In 1949, the newspaper won the public service Pulitzer Prize for its crusade to establish a bipartisan committee to spotlight issues early in the presidential campaign. In 1946, Joe W. and his sons, Joe R. and James C. (Jim), purchased the *North Platte Telegraph* and the North Platte Publishing Company,[148] which owned the *North Platte Bulletin*. With the merger of the two papers, the *Telegraph-Bulletin* was born. The family eventually would own and operate four newspapers in Nebraska: the *North Platte Telegraph*, the *Scottsbluff Star-Herald*, the *Lexington Clipper-Herald* and the *Sidney Telegraph*, until selling it to the *Omaha World-Herald* in 2000.

Joe R. Seacrest joined the *Lincoln Journal* editorial staff in 1946. He received his law degree in 1949 and soon became the courthouse reporter. He was managing editor of the *Lincoln Journal* from 1958 to 1973 and editor from 1973 until 1986.

James (Jim) Seacrest and his wife, Rhonda. *Blackledge Collection.*

Joe R.'s younger brother, Jim, arrived at the *North Platte Telegraph* in 1966 at the age of twenty-eight to learn the newspaper business. Seacrest worked in virtually every department of the paper, including in the newsroom as a reporter under Blackledge, from whom he said he really learned journalism.[149] Jim Seacrest later became the newspaper's publisher and was president and chairman of the board of the company.[150]

It didn't take Blackledge long to realize that the Seacrests were technological trendsetters. Joe R. was an early adopter of the latest equipment because he wanted to produce a quality newspaper as rapidly and efficiently as possible.

To that end, the *North Platte Telegraph* would turn out to be a technological pioneer.[151] And the new editor not only embraced the technology but also kept the *Telegraph* readers informed with the addition of each innovation.

When the *Telegraph* published the first run of its new high-speed web offset press on June 10, 1968, Blackledge schooled readers about how getting news into print was changing. As he told them, offset transformed the labor-intensive—and dirty—typesetting process. Blackledge compared the change from hot metal to offset like shifting from a horse-drawn plow to a tractor or from a steam engine to diesel. "We are excited about the shiny new equipment that is so different from the grease-and-ink-stained stuff that we have loved and hated for so long," he said.[152]

Joe R. also appreciated computers, especially their word storage capabilities, which meant that news stories eventually would be edited without retyping. To that end, in the mid-1970s, the *Telegraph* began the process of phasing out scanners, to be replaced by computers called video display terminals (VDTs). Again, Blackledge described the change to readers. For several years, he explained, scanners were used to translate the reporters' typewritten copy directly onto punched tape that fed into a phototypesetting machine, producing the type to be pasted on the finished page. With the new technology, reporters type their stories on VDTs, where the copy appears on a television-type screen instead of paper. The stories are transferred to another computer terminal for editing or stored for later editing.[153]

By the time Blackledge had returned to North Platte in 1967, *Bulletin* had been dropped from the paper's name. The *Telegraph* was still at its East Fifth Street location, although over the years the newsroom had moved from upstairs to downstairs, later upstairs and then downstairs again.

The new editor quickly settled into his very own office and began juggling the myriad tasks that came almost immediately with the position. Meanwhile, as the news staff watched, Blackledge almost daily lugged into his office several large binders that held old *Telegraph-Bulletin* and *Telegraph* newspapers. The books that contained the bound volumes of broadsheet newspapers measured some thirty by twenty-four inches, and Blackledge was combing through the editorials and opinion pieces from the 1930s onward to determine the paper's previous editorial positions. In a file folder, thick with pages of Blackledge's handwritten notes, Blackledge wrote that the newspaper largely avoided local editorial posturing until about 1965, when a policy began to evolve and local editorials were written with more regularity. The editor went on to note the newspaper's stance on a variety of topics, including taxation and spending, North Platte and regional development, agriculture, education, law enforcement, federal aid (the *Telegraph* was not opposed to using federal money to help the city), public access to information and city development.

Joe R. wanted local editorials every day, and Blackledge provided them. He varied the topics, kept the focus on North Platte and frequently used humor to make a point. For example, readers were told about the wreckage in the *Telegraph*'s main office during a major remodeling project undertaken about a year after the new editor arrived. As Blackledge described the place, desks had been moved to accommodate the crisscrossing of trenches for new utility wires and pipes with "little bridges built across the trenches so that women employees could get from desk to desk without getting (much) sand in their shoes."[154] A fine layer of cement dust had settled over everything. But there were advantages:

> *The editor's desk, once the worst-looking area in the building, became at least as neat as anyplace else....People come in to complain, look around, shake their heads in wonderment and leave, forgetting what it was they wanted to complain about.*[155]

Readers also got the inside scoop after the *Telegraph*'s canoe capsized while shooting photos of the annual Jaycees' canoe race down the North Platte River:

> *In case you haven't heard, we lost a camera with a zoom telephoto lens and our film (plus some shoes, two pairs of glasses, socks, and two ham and cheese sandwiches) to the rushing waters of the Platte. From the fire department comes an offer of a Brownie camera....And a local professional photographic dealer, who handles the type of camera which was lost, offers special cut prices plus canoe lessons for a volume camera purchase.*[156]

When North Platte opened its first one-way streets on the Jeffers-Dewey routes to and from the interstate on September 5, 1968—which the *Telegraph* supported—the editor didn't hesitate to reprimand state and local officials for not forewarning the citizens:

> *Someone you would think might have thought that such a major change in traffic pattern deserved a public announcement, at least the day before it happened....The conviction grows that the people concerned with highways and streets consider the driver last.*[157]

In a 2010 interview, Blackledge remembered those first few years as editor of the *Telegraph*:

> *I wrote an editorial every day and a column on Sundays and edited most of the local copy and some of the wire copy. I worked like hell for several years and inherited the staff that needed some improvement. I gradually improved the staff. Never had any second guessing from Seacrest....It was the next best thing to owning your own newspaper, maybe better because I didn't have to spend a lot of time worrying about the profit and loss on the revenue.* [158]

According to publisher Jim Seacrest, "Keith was a man ahead of his time. He was very talented....He had his own mind about things, his own objectives, and sometimes it worked, sometimes it didn't." [159] When it didn't work, Blackledge understood that too:

> *Many times members of the Seacrest family took the heat from their own friends and associates for ideas expressed on the editorial page which were not their ideas and which in some cases were the opposite of what they would have said. Once in a while they winced, but they never complained. Offended readers who sought to go over the editor's head were politely but firmly rebuffed.* [160]

One time Blackledge took on the North Platte School Board and its attorney, Harold Kay, in his editorials after the school superintendent was charged and later convicted of misdemeanor third-degree sexual assault. [161] Blackledge was critical of the board on several counts: the board's votes on matters relating to the controversy—without discussion—which clearly had taken place during previous closed sessions or informal get-togethers, as well as the board's failure to secure legal counsel from outside North Platte because attorney Kay and the school administrator were friends.

Blackledge was particularly concerned about the school board's lack of commitment to openness when, following an important vote, "there was no discussion on how or why the board arrived at its decisions." He noted such action "deprives the public of any insight into how decisions are reached and whether or not contrary points of view were considered." [162]

Regarding the attorney and school official's friendship, Blackledge warned that the board risked losing credibility. Without trust, he said, the board would be unable to assure the public that its actions relating to the superintendent's legal dilemma were thorough and objective:

> *This is no reflection on the board's present attorney. It is simply recognition that in the nature of their jobs, the attorney and the superintendent have had frequent association over a long period of time. If there is any personal relationship at all, it could be a handicap to impartial action. And even if the attorney is capable of separating his personal feelings from his professional judgment, there is the problem of convincing the public that he has done so.*[163]

In an editorial a few days later, Blackledge took issue with Kay's charge that the *Telegraph* was trying the case against the superintendent in the newspaper, noting that comment had been withheld for more than a month to avoid impeding the superintendent's chances for a fair trial.[164]

Years later, Kay described Blackledge as "a smart guy and good writer... who was so good for the town." He added, "We had our clashes on things. But I always respected him, and I think he respected me."[165]

Blackledge also had clashes with the publisher. For instance, there was the time the editor wanted to delay the early morning press run of the Sunday edition to wait on a late-breaking story. The press foreman refused, and Seacrest stepped in. Concerned about the havoc wreaked on deliveries the delay would cause, the publisher ruled for running the presses on time. "Keith was not happy," Seacrest said with a chuckle.[166]

It wouldn't be the last skirmish the publisher and editor would have, but over time, their mutual respect deepened and a lifelong friendship between the two newspapermen grew.

When the Inland Press Association twice presented Blackledge first-place awards in the William Allen White Editorial Excellence competition—first in 1977 and again in 1985—and the topmost Editorial Excellence Sweepstakes Award in 1981, the Seacrests were among his most ardent supporters.[167] Jim and his wife, Rhonda, twice accompanied Blackledge to the association's annual Chicago conference, where the awards were announced. "What paper? The *North Platte Telegraph*. Where the hell is that?" Seacrest imagined many thinking.[168]

In a reminiscent mood several years before his retirement, Blackledge reiterated his admiration for the community journalist from Emporia, Kansas: "William Allen White was a small-town editor with a national and world view, who at the same time was deeply involved and an activist within his own community. Consciously and subconsciously, his was a pattern I tried to follow."[169]

Yet community journalism is not without its detractors. While some scholars praise community journalism as the only approach left for newspapers to save themselves from extinction, there is criticism: community journalism's overemphasis on civic commitment overshadows its watchdog role; community journalism fails to deal with major community problems; and objectivity—that almost sacrosanct journalistic guiding principle—is the antithesis of community journalism.[170]

But people who worked with Keith Blackledge tell a different story. Not long after Blackledge became the *Telegraph* editor, Eric Seacrest joined the news staff as wire and copy editor. "Keith never sold out for any cause. Keith always reported the news accurately—accuracy was paramount." he said. "But as an editorialist he could advocate for whatever cause he thought was beneficial to the community."[171] Seacrest, now executive director of the Mid-Nebraska Community Foundation, and Blackledge worked together on numerous community projects over the years. "Did Keith make people mad? Absolutely. He didn't go out of his way to do so, but if that was the consequence of telling the truth, he could live with it," Seacrest remarked.[172]

Judy Nelson, general assignments and agriculture reporter and later news editor at the *Telegraph* from 1972 to 1975, said that Blackledge taught his staff to report the truth. "The facts, he said, will give people the opportunity to know the problem," she remembered him preaching, adding that he wasn't afraid of taking on unpopular issues.[173]

Sharron Hollen, whose career at the *Telegraph* spanned decades from the early 1960s and well into the 2000s, said that Blackledge was skillful at balancing his love of North Platte with good journalism. "He was well-respected, but his focus was always on the news. He was a man who could not be manipulated."[174]

Jill Claflin, former *Telegraph* copy editor and managing editor, also talked about Blackledge's ability to negotiate community journalism and objectivism. "Keith Blackledge," she said, "was not objective about North Platte at all. He was a champion of the town, but at the same time he championed accountability."[175] She described him as both cheerleader and stalwart newspaperman.[176]

Dan Moser succeeded Blackledge as the *Telegraph*'s executive editor in 1991 after some eight years as a reporter and eventually managing editor on the news staff. According to Moser, Blackledge believed that if a community succeeds, the newspaper succeeds. "But he also understood that we are not here to boost, but to cover," Moser noted, explaining that he knew this about his editor not because of what he said, but by the decisions he made.[177] The *Telegraph*'s editorial page was a force behind major community endeavors, yet the news pages remained objective:

Keith used his editorials and columns as a bully pulpit, but he never expected a positive slant to the coverage. The Telegraph *was not a Chamber of Commerce newspaper. And I have to believe Keith took a good deal of grief from the Chamber of Commerce and many others. You would see people— sometimes very angry people—come into his office, and you knew what they were there for.*[178]

Moser said that covering their editor's many causes and community projects could be challenging for the news staff. And Moser added that he inevitably would have to do stories about something the editor was passionate about. Case in point: the unsuccessful effort to land a Federal Aviation Administration Flight Service Center in North Platte when the FAA was closing its more than three hundred existing flight service centers across the country to be replaced by sixty-one highly automated regional facilities. Throughout the summer and into the winter of 1983, while North Platte was preparing the bid to submit to the FAA, Moser wrote the news stories and Blackledge's editorials supported the initiative.

Eventually, the FAA rejected North Platte's proposal and picked Columbus as home for the new flight service center. Moser soon discovered that North Platte had been eliminated because its application had been botched. "It was really a civic embarrassment because the community had pushed so much for this," Moser recalled.[179]

At the late afternoon editors' planning meeting the day the decision was announced, Blackledge told Moser that the story should run across the top of page one. Moser's lead of the story read, "North Platte was not considered as a site for Nebraska's automated flight service center because it did not comply with bidding guidelines, an FAA official said."[180] After the story was published, Moser said that Blackledge approached him at his desk with the comment, "That was a good story." And off he went![181]

As Blackledge once explained:

A reporter's job is to gather information and report it as completely, as accurately and as fairly as possible. An editor's job is to help the reporter decide what, out of all that limitless supply of news ought to be reported in the first place; check to see that it is reported accurately, completely, and fairly, and then, perhaps, to comment upon it on the editorial page. A newspaper that gives its readers only the news may be adequate, but it is only giving its readers a part of what a newspaper can be.[182]

Not long after his retirement, the man who brought Blackledge back to North Platte, Joe R. Seacrest, described the community service function of newspapers in terms of agenda setting, which posits that the media—in this case the local newspaper—do not tell people what to think, but rather what to think about.[183] Agenda setting is a way to explain how the media help shape public opinion through their selection of and the importance they place on the news of the day. As Joe R. Seacrest explained it, the role of the press as an agenda setter is in "realizing what the substantial questions are, pointing out problems and possible alternatives, and in airing public debate in the merits and demerits of all possible solutions so that the democratic process can operate."[184]

In 1967, Joe R. had found just the right newspaperman. Keith Blackledge was the archetypal community journalist, ever vigilant at identifying ways to improve the town he loved. And for a quarter of a century, Blackledge used persuasion in his editorials and columns, and he rallied those with the courage and desire to make things happen.[185]

Chapter 5

MAKING THINGS HAPPEN

*I've learned some things from my own experience. I've known that no newspaper
"crusade" brings results unless there are people behind it. Publicity or editorials
alone won't raise money for a worthy cause, or pass a bond issue, or bring on
a needed reform unless there are citizens working in an organized way to make
something happen. Sometimes an editor has to get out of the office and help
organize those citizens.*
—*Keith Blackledge*[186]

ollowing long-standing family tradition, *North Platte Telegraph* owner
Joe R. Seacrest believed that "community service was the reason for
newspapers, and advertising paid to make that happen."[187] When Keith
Blackledge came to town in 1967 as the newspaper's new executive editor, he
was eager to make things happen in North Platte. Like William Allen White,
the Emporia, Kansas community journalist he so admired, Blackledge's
position at the *Telegraph* would far exceed reporting the news. "Blackledge
rallied the community for a cause, he was passionate about North Platte,
and, whatever the issue the community faced, Blackledge formed an opinion
and wrote about it."[188]

Blackledge's return to the *Telegraph* came one hundred years after the
town's modest beginnings. Railroad construction had reached the site of
what would become North Platte in 1866; however, when Union Pacific
changed its terminus to Julesburg, Colorado, in 1867, most of the town's
inhabitants pulled up stakes with the railroad. The village of some several

thousand decreased to about three hundred.[189] But according to Blackledge, "North Platte was more or less on the map. Gen. Grenville Dodge of the Union Pacific had laid out a town site in 1866, and the plat was filed with the clerk of the county court in January, 1867."[190]

Residents moved the county seat from Cottonwood Springs to North Platte in an election on October 8, 1867—just twenty-one votes were cast. It was a start though. School District I was organized in 1868, with private donations funding the first log schoolhouse, located at what is now Fifth and Dewey Streets. North Platte was incorporated in 1873.[191]

When Blackledge returned to the *Telegraph* in 1967, the clash between North Platte and McCook over the establishment of vocational technical schools and junior colleges in the state's west-central region had reached fever pitch. Two strong newspaper editors—Blackledge and Allen Strunk[192] of the *McCook Gazette*—battled it out in their respective editorial pages. "It was the sort of combat a newspaper editor could relish, generating lots of copy and recalling the journalism of another era when editors of rival newspapers exchanged arguments and insults."[193]

The conflict centered on the legislature's efforts to provide equitable postsecondary, two-year educational opportunities for its residents. In North Platte, it all began in 1961, when voters established a junior college district. The 1913 post office was remodeled to serve as quarters for the new school.[194]

In 1965, the Nebraska Unicameral passed legislation so localities could create multi-county districts to establish two-year vocational trade schools. Back then, the only such school in the state was at Milford. At that time, the technical schools focused on vocational training, while the two-year junior colleges concentrated on academics.

Voters in west-central Nebraska approved a ten-county vocational trade school district in 1966. North Platte would house the Mid-Plains Technical School. But seven counties, including Red Willow (McCook), fought for the next two years for exclusion from the district. Thus, by the time Blackledge arrived in town, North Platte had been working to get the school up and running, while McCook was intensifying efforts to kill it. As the battle roiled, words like *vendetta*, *unconstitutional* and *liars* were commonly seen in the *Gazette* and *Telegraph* opinion pages. "We exchanged editorials as well as letters. *Gazette* subscribers could read some of my arguments for the school and *Telegraph* subscribers could read Strunk's arguments against. There is no evidence we changed anyone's mind in either town."[195]

In 1968, the effort to withdraw from Mid-Plains Vocational Technical District failed, making North Platte the official home of the trade school, where students already were participating in technical programs in two rented facilities. Other postsecondary students continued to take junior college classes in the renovated post office.[196]

Meanwhile, the line between technical schools and junior colleges was blurring. In 1971, the legislature directed the state's hodgepodge of junior colleges and trade schools to merge within multi-county districts. North Platte and McCook eventually were brought into the Mid-Plains Community College District. But the postsecondary two-year college dispute didn't end there. The disagreement had shifted, this time among North Platte's citizens. Should there be one campus or two, and where should the school be located?

Finally, in 1973, the North Platte junior college and vocational tech school combined boards, and the two-campus proponents finally won the day. The original trade school would become known as Mid-Nebraska Community College's North Campus and the original community college South Campus.[197]

As Blackledge observed, "Some of our greatest institutions including our country itself, have had beginnings under difficult circumstances. Courageous, dedicated men brought them into existence in spite of, or perhaps because of, these initial obstacles."[198]

In the meantime, another controversy was pulling the community apart and the editor into the fray. For years, North Platte had two small and increasingly tired hospitals: St. Mary and Memorial. In 1969, Memorial Hospital announced the launch of a $500,000 fund drive for a new forty-

Mid-Plains Community College campus. *MPCCA.*

two-bed facility. Within weeks, at the urging of *Telegraph* publisher Jim Kirkman and Blackledge, the Mayor's Hospital Planning Council was set up to review community health needs, while Memorial Hospital held off on its fundraising. A New York State consulting firm, brought in to study the region's hospital situation, ultimately recommended consolidating the two hospitals.[199] The long-range goal was to build a single modern medical facility. But the prickly healthcare battle had only just begun.

While Blackledge's editorials enthusiastically supported the one-hospital concept, opponents kept up their protests, filling the letters-to-editor columns. On January 29, 1973, Blackledge's editorial, titled "The Prejudice that Blinds," was published in response to three North Platte physicians' appearance on a local television program to denounce the hospital merger plan. Blackledge wrote:

> *A new show made its debut on local television last night. It might have been called "The Three Blind Mice."...It is sad and a little frightening that three men who are so useful in their professions and so personable as individuals can be so short of vision in matters of community effort.... Their case consisted of a few arguments, a few questions, most of which have been answered, and a lot of innuendo.*[200]

One of the "mice" was the physician of *Telegraph* assistant editor Bill Eddy, who'd been hospitalized with a bout of pneumonia around the time Blackledge's editorial was published. When the doctor came into Eddy's room, he pulled up a chair and said, "Bill, let's talk." Chuckling, Eddy recalled, "Keith's editorial made my doctor want to talk politics—at my bedside."[201]

Did the column change the doctors' minds? Not likely.

On July 18, 1973, a page-one *Telegraph* headline proclaimed, "North Platte Hospital Fund Tops Goal." The Great Plains Medical Center building was dedicated on August 9, 1975, climaxing an effort that had begun in 1969. "Regional" would later be added to the name.

As a colleague and friend of Blackledge described the editor's strategy: "Keith wrote the articles, columns, editorials, and then held the coattails for others to do the work on the ground."[202] Or, as one *Telegraph* reporter observed:

> *Keith would pick up the phone to call one of the civic leaders in town—he knew them all—to say, "Let's have lunch tomorrow." That person surely*

Left: Newspaperman and editor Bill Eddy. *North Platte Telegraph.*

Below: The grand opening of Great Plains Regional Medical Center in 1975. *GPRMC.*

knew by the end of the meal, he or she soon would be forking over money or heading up some committee.[203]

It was a strategy Blackledge used from the time he returned to North Platte in 1967 and years beyond his retirement in 1992. Blackledge's book *That Town Fights about Everything* provides a detailed account of North Platte's many battles.

Blackledge's first involvement in a school bond initiative ended in disappointment when voters rejected a proposal in 1971 to replace the forty-year-old high school. Undeterred, however, Blackledge soon led editorial and personal support on a $10 million bond measure, which voters approved on October 21, 1975, to replace the 1948 junior high, build one elementary school and renovate several other schools.[204]

In the meantime, the town continued to grapple with growing school enrollments and an aging senior high. The imposing three-story North Platte High School opened doors in 1930, with updates in 1964 and 1975. By the early 1990s, it was clear that the high school needed replacing, but proposals to build a new school would face ballot rejection in 1993, 1994 and 1997.[205] Blackledge supported replacing the old school each and every time.

After the failed 1997 bond election, one of the more strident opponents proposed a volunteer effort to spruce up the old school. Blackledge supported the idea editorially and wrote a letter to the organizer with suggestions for marshaling volunteers. His eight-point list of recommendations included ways to prioritize tasks, designate job supervisors and make the work enjoyable. "There could be music from high school band members at intervals in the hallways. The Bulldog mascot could be drafted. T-shirts for each volunteer? Name tags?" he wrote. Before signing off on the letter—complete with names and phone numbers of potential volunteers—Blackledge modestly stated, "I'm sure you've thought of all of these things and more. Thanks for getting this started."[206]

On the day of the cleanup, fifteen people arrived at the school with rags, brooms and brushes—including Blackledge, who said, "Of course, I had to show up and do some painting myself."[207] Years later, the man who proposed the work project wrote to Blackledge, stating that the editor wasn't as bad a guy as he'd imagined.

Blackledge loved history. To that end, many of his initiatives focused on preserving North Platte's past. In a column in 1958 titled "Pipe Dream Department," the editor suggested that local history would best be served by reviving the long-dead Lincoln County Historical Society.[208] When Blackledge left North Platte a year later, the pipe dream was no closer to reality. His successor, Ted Turpin, kept the idea afloat, and the Lincoln County Historical Society was resurrected in 1960. Upon Blackledge's return in 1967, he endorsed establishing a permanent place to house the society's collection of historic items, being stored mostly in members' garages. The Lincoln County Historical Museum was dedicated on July 4, 1976. Blackledge also backed the effort to save the William Jeffers House, which for years sat vacant and deteriorating in Cody Park. Now a popular visitors' site, the home of the North Platte's Union Pacific magnate was moved to the museum grounds in 2000.

Many ventures to preserve the town's history were met with skepticism and others outright hostility. When an additional 233 acres became available in 1987 to develop campgrounds and accommodations for recreation vehicles at Buffalo Bill Ranch State Historical Park, opposition came largely from the Lincoln County Lodging Association. Blackledge, who editorially favored the plan, remembered, "The owner of a private campground accused me of trying to put him out of business."[209] Proponents prevailed, and the recreation area was dedicated on June 3, 2000. The private campground remains in operation today.

Some years later, Blackledge headed the committee exploring ways to commemorate Union Pacific's historic presence in North Platte. In 1999, plans were announced to seek funds for a 150-foot edifice at the Union Pacific Bailey Yard. The campaign was plagued by disagreement concerning the acquisition of loans, a possible occupancy tax and the structure's design. It took almost a decade, during which time donations were meager, leaders squabbled and feelings got hurt, but supporters pressed on.[210] The grand opening ceremony for Gold Spike Tower and Visitor Center was held on June 6, 2008.

One of Blackledge's biggest disappointments was the demolition of the old Union Pacific depot, home to the famous North Platte World War II Canteen. While the effort to save the old depot was generally supported, the battle this time was with the railroad. The Canteen began on Christmas Day 1941, after the sister of a Nebraska National Guard member organized the delivery of Christmas baskets for the Company D unit when the train came through town. Instead of Nebraskans, a contingent from Kansas was on board, but townspeople presented gifts to the soldiers anyway.[211]

For fifty-one months, millions of service men and women riding the troop trains were greeted, cheered and served food in a continuous 'round-the-clock operation that depended on thousands of volunteers from 125 communities in Nebraska and Colorado. "At its best, it is a grand story of giving—Canteen workers who gave so freely of their time, their rationed food; soldiers who gave years of their lives and were willing to give their lives."[212]

The Canteen sign came down from the door of the depot on April 1, 1946. After passenger service ended in 1971, a campaign to save the building began. But the railroad couldn't be convinced to preserve the old structure. Constructed in 1918, it was razed in 1973. A public mini-park was dedicated in 1975 at the site of the Canteen at milepost 284.1. The defeat served to increase Blackledge's lifelong commitment to historic preservation.

Throughout the years, Blackledge's columns and editorials kept the Canteen story alive. In 1994, the Lincoln County Historical Museum hosted a reception for the World War II Canteen volunteers—the oldest in attendance was 101. When nationally syndicated columnist Bob Greene began research on a book about the Canteen, the Chicago newspaperman and the retired North Platte editor became friends. Greene, who dedicated the book *Once Upon a Town: The Miracle of the North Platte Canteen* to Blackledge, wrote:

> *Mr. Blackledge's friendship toward me, his endless patience with my questions, his willingness to walk me through various aspects of North Platte's past…all were indispensable to my work. His love of, and uncompromisingly high standards for his town are evident in everything he does.*[213]

Blackledge's disappointment didn't end with the loss of the depot. In the summer of 1971, Monte Montana Jr.'s reenactment of Buffalo Bill's Original Wild West Show opened in the new NEBRASKAland Days Wild West Arena.[214] But public response was lackluster. The season opened on June 13, 1974, amid much fanfare, with 1950s canine celebrity Lassie's guest appearance.[215] Still, ticket sales and sponsorships remained flat, and after the second season, the Wild West Show was unable to continue. Blackledge and the newspaper had backed the show.

Undaunted, organizers came up with another concept. The Wild West World Musical ran nightly at the arena during the summer of 1975. Gary Toebben,[216] then president of the chamber of commerce, worked with Blackledge to promote the show. Blackledge, besides investing his own money, played a major role in raising funds throughout Lincoln County. But the Wild West World Musical met with the same fate as its predecessor, losing about $200,000 from local backers. Blackledge took that one particularly hard.[217]

Then came another blow. The Nebraska Midland Railroad, powered by a 1908 Baldwin steam-fired locomotive and a thirteen-unit collection of 1874–1908 vintage rolling stock cars, operated briefly on a small line of track near Buffalo Bill Ranch State Historical Park in summer 1973. But plans that the train traverse a route between the state park and Cody Park were derailed when right-of-way negotiations failed.[218] The Nebraska Midland Railroad departed North Platte's Victoria Station for the last time en route to Grand Island's Stuhr Museum in the fall of 1975. "Our town let it slip away through misunderstanding, bad timing and misdirection of our tourism efforts....The *Telegraph* tried to stir some interest in saving the railroad for North Platte, but nothing stirred. We might have done more," Blackledge lamented.[219]

Many townspeople also remember the initiative to install a fountain in a lake south of the brand-new Interstate 80 near North Platte in 1975. It was referred to by many as "Fontane's Folly" because City Councilman Bruno Albert Fontane's idea seemed so implausible to the critics. Blackledge threw his editorial (and financial) support behind the effort, suggesting the name Bicentennial Fountain to mark the nation's 1976 bicentennial year.[220] While the debate played out in the *Telegraph*'s opinion pages, Fontane pushed on. Eventually, some $10,000 was raised, and Blackledge's name suggestion stuck—Bicentennial Fountain became a reality. City crews dutifully installed the fountain in the lake each spring and removed it each fall. But beset by lighting and spray problems, the fountain fizzled and was moved to Cody Park pond. Some years later, in need of repair, Bicentennial Fountain was removed and never replaced.[221]

Blackledge had backed the successful $29 million bond election in 2000 to build a new high school; however, he soon became entangled in the controversy about what to do with the old school. Save it or tear it down? The issue divided the town—and the Blackledges.

From 1997 through 2004, Blackledge's middle son, optometrist Mark A. Blackledge, served on the board of education. Dr. Blackledge was president of the board in 2002 when the battle to save the old high school building intensified. The senior Blackledge, long retired from the *Telegraph* by then, was a proponent of saving the section of the building that had first been a basketball court and then a fine arts theater. The idea was to turn that part of the building into a public library.

At the meeting when the school board was to vote on the building's fate, people for demolition (like Dr. Blackledge's mother, Jo Ann) sat on one side of the room and those opposed (among them his father, Keith Blackledge) the other. Tensions were high as threats and insults hurled from one side to the other; police were on hand anticipating trouble. "This will not be a good Christmas for me," quipped Dr. Blackledge, before casting his vote to raze the structure.[222]

In 2003, the high school was demolished. "The thought of tearing down the 1930s building to make way for a parking lot or a tennis court makes the editor roll his eyes," Blackledge wrote.[223]

Not all projects produced conflict, although fundraising on most was perpetually challenging—that's when Blackledge often would step in. For example, the attempt to save the old city-owned post office building. When the idea to turn the Italian Renaissance structure into city hall didn't pan out, the Creativity Unlimited Arts Council offered plans in 2007 to convert it into an art center. After a slow start, Blackledge was brought in to organize and lead the effort to raise money. The Prairie Arts Center opened its doors in 2008. This would be one of the editor's final initiatives.[224]

Blackledge's community activism began long before the junior college and trade school battles heated up, the hospital merger polarized the town, the perennial fights over school bond requests or the many efforts to save the town's history. In the 1954 election year, newspaperman Jim Kirkman invited the young Blackledge to meetings organized to recruit and support qualified candidates for public office. The committee had roots in the 1951 election after Kirk Mendenhall, the new mayor, was closing down the town's decades-old gambling dens and bordellos.[225] Kirkman, then the newspaper's advertising manager, designed the ads supporting the reform movement and at some point during this time spearheaded the election committee.

According to Blackledge, "That was a great education on how things sometimes get done—and sometimes don't—in a small town."[226] When he returned to North Platte in 1967, Blackledge resumed ties to the group, by then called the Candidate Committee for City Government.

The loosely structured committee included local business and professional people. Once a potential candidate was vetted and agreed to run, a campaign committee helped candidates identify and become versed on key issues, wrote letters, made calls, planned the budget and raised money. Candidates typically ran for city council, county board or school board, as well as contended for county offices or state legislative seats from the Forty-Second District.[227]

Former mayor Jim Whitaker.
David Whitaker.

Longtime friend Jim Whitaker met Blackledge at one of the committee meetings.[228] "I liked Keith right away. He didn't talk much but when he did, you knew he had something important to say."[229] Whitaker often referred to Blackledge as "Mr. Somebody" because the editor was "the Somebody" people sought out to lead a cause.

Whitaker said that he was aware that some folks referred to the Candidate Committee as good ol' boys. "Not so!" he declared. "This was not a quid pro quo sort of thing; we really wanted to get the best candidates we could."[230]

One such candidate was Whitaker himself, whom the committee convinced to run for mayor. He went on to serve two terms from 1996 to 2004. At Whitaker's retirement celebration in 2005, Blackledge read the editorial published in honor of the mayor's service to the town. Whitaker recalled the reading. "Keith paused for quite a long time toward the end. Then he said, 'I always choke up when I read my own material.' He got a good laugh."[231]

Not all Blackledge initiatives were met with acrimony; not all were big and expensive. Like the marigolds. Here's how he urged readers to plant the flowers in one of his earlier columns in the mid-1980s:

> *Think if each business operator were to plant each available parkway with marigolds in place of weeds. The impact of all that bright color upon visitors entering or leaving North Platte would be striking, and would do much to overcome the general impression now of drabness and neglect.*[232]

Every spring, for more than ten years, the editor toured the town and editorially reprimanded businesses with untidy and weed-invested grounds and parking lots. Gibson's discount store gave out hundreds of marigolds, and Lexington resident Jack Ragsdale donated thousands of flowers until he moved to California in 1987. The beautification scheme continued nonetheless, with merchants and residents working from early spring to fall weeding and watering the flower plots. Every August, Blackledge toured the city again, this time paying tribute to the businesses that had spruced up the landscaping. Blackledge once admitted that he wrote about marigolds whenever he couldn't think of anything else to write about.[233]

Blackledge said that getting the new band organ for the Cody Park carousel was one of his easiest crusades. The carousel has something of an up-and-down history. Sometime in the late 1940s or early 1950s a local Union Pacific machinist installed the restored early 1900s carousel in Cody Park. In 1969, Jack Sawyer of Roscoe, Nebraska, bought the carousel, but three years later he was in negotiations for its purchase with the Ogallala City Council. But the deal fell through, and Sawyer continued the operation until 1975, when the City of North Platte purchased the carousel for $15,000.[234]

During the off-season, park employees cleaned and repaired the carousel and its twenty-four original horses. But because a player organ had not been part of the initial purchase, the authentic carousel sound was missing. Instead, Sawyer played tapes of merry-go-round music; later, the steeds pranced to recorded rock and country music amplified through concession booth loudspeakers.[235]

Dedication of the Cody Park carousel band organ in 2004. *From left to right*: Jim and Rhonda Seacrest and Keith and Mary Ann Blackledge. *Blackledge family.*

Only 173 antique carousels remained on the North American continent, Blackledge told readers. "But it needs music to be complete," he wrote. "We hope that some way can be found to add merry-go-round music to the wonderful Cody Park merry-go-round."[236]

Then came the $21,500 donation from Jim Seacrest, former *Telegraph* publisher, and his wife, Rhonda, who rode the carousel in Cody Park as a child.[237] The new band organ was dedicated on May 29, 2004. For years, a proud Blackledge took visitors to see and hear the Cody Park carousel.

By the 1980s, some of Blackledge's excursions out of the *Telegraph* office took him away from North Platte. Friend and former Nebraska secretary of state John Gale[238] said Blackledge was one of the few people he knew who was interested in developing a relationship between eastern and western Nebraska, as well as bridging the state's urban and rural gap. "Keith held a rare vision of a unified Nebraska—and he nurtured that climate by providing solid leadership on statewide committees, commissions, and boards."[239]

Blackledge served on the Nebraska State Colleges Board of Trustees from 1987 to 1993. Testifying on February 21, 1989, before the Nebraska legislature's Education Committee concerning the proposal that Kearney State College leave the state college system to become part of the University of Nebraska, he stated:

> *I think my feeling about Kearney State is something like that of a father whose favorite daughter has announced plans to marry and leave home. I am naturally reluctant to see her go....I wish that her lover showed a little more enthusiasm for the match. I do not want a shotgun wedding. I expect he can offer her some things I cannot, but if he restricts her and breaks her spirit to get her to conform to his style, it will be a bad marriage.*[240]

Blackledge's remarks drew widespread praise. Kearney State College moved into the university system in 1991.

Shortly after joining the Nebraska Educational Telecommunications NET Commission in 1994, Blackledge complained that no refreshments were provided during meetings, remembered Rodney Bates, retired general manager of NET.[241] Soon the so-called Blackledge Memorial Snack Bar was instituted featuring homemade chocolate chip cookies—Blackledge's favorite—and coffee.[242] As a board member of the Public Radio Nebraska Foundation and the NET Commission and a longtime advocate for a statewide educational broadcasting network, Blackledge was in on the groundwork as both boards created Nebraska's public radio and television networks. Blackledge's editorials helped build support, especially in the western part of the state.[243]

Blackledge's last statewide initiative was the push for tax incentives for historical preservation. Amendment 1 was signed into Nebraska law in 2005. "How Keith managed to drive all of those highway miles, take the time that he did, and fulfill all of his responsibilities at home is extraordinary," remarked Gale.[244]

But fulfill them he did. As longtime Nebraska journalist Ed Howard[245] observed:

> *If parents looked after their kids the way Blackledge has tried to look after North Platte, delinquency statistics would nosedive faster than the 2004 Husker football team. And, in some ways, even an old community is like a youngster. It is often going in a lot of directions and it can be helped with a bit of guidance. Keith Blackledge has been North Platte's guidance counselor ex officio for decades.*[246]

Chapter 6

THE WORDSMITH AND HIS NEWSROOM

It is not hard to write an editorial, just as it is not hard to write.
Everyone can do both—until they have to.
—Keith Blackledge[247]

While community initiatives frequently got the editor out of the office, Keith Blackledge spent most days tending to the business of putting out a daily newspaper—and writing. He wrote his "Your Town and Mine" column for more than forty years and an editorial almost daily for a quarter of a century for the *North Platte Telegraph*.

Legendary as a man of few words, Blackledge revealed himself through his writing. For example, readers learned that their editor liked Mark Twain and William Allen White, cool summer evenings, chocolate chip cookies and community. They also knew that he hated ignorance, cold gray winters and verbosity—not because he said so, but from what he wrote. He could deftly string words together to form sentences. He was a master summarizer of ideas. He was a wordsmith who did not mince them.

An early riser, Blackledge finished his morning ablutions by daylight, arriving in the newsroom around 7:30 a.m. before anyone else—before the spirited news staffers began filtering in, before the incessant ringing of phones, the meetings, the deadlines and the readers who frequently dropped in unannounced, typically with grievances and occasionally a compliment. Blackledge listened to them all—his office door was seldom closed—sitting at his desk cluttered with papers and file folders, a well-worn Rolodex at his fingertips. More papers, files, books and newspapers were piled on chairs and around the office perimeter. Despite the disarray, Blackledge said that he could always find what he needed.[248] The editor's philosophy, "I wouldn't like to have lived without ever having disturbed anyone," hung on a wall near the desk.

Fridays were special for the editorial department. Late in the afternoon, the staff gathered for the news meeting. Blackledge sat at one end of the conference table, with the team situated around him on both sides. Coffee cups, pop cans and various snack items littered the table. Occasionally home-baked cookies added to the fare. Reporters received copies of the previous week's papers with their published stories marked up with editing symbols and Blackledge's notations. The editor led the discussion. Do you think readers understood your explanation of the mill levy rate? Why didn't you lead off the story with the information in the fourth graf? Are you satisfied with the way this story flowed? Do you know the difference between *affect* and *effect*, *its* and *it's*? Rather than providing answers, reporters were encouraged to rethink some stories, whether in terms of the information presented—too much or too little—or the decisions made while writing and editing. In addition to the critiques, Blackledge and the staff talked about upcoming news events and planned the coverage.[249]

During high school sports seasons, Friday nights were particularly hectic as coaches from throughout the twenty-two-county area phoned in scores and game highlights. Everyone in the editorial department and sometimes their family members, plus numerous part-timers and high school journalism students, worked Friday nights to take the calls. When the paper went to press, the regular news staff trooped to the White Horse, a bar about a block from the *Telegraph*, to unwind. Staffers affectionately called the White Horse the newspaper annex.

Blackledge often said that he spent a lot of time thinking about, researching, writing and polishing his daily editorials and weekly columns. Indeed, he believed his commentaries offered him the best chance to connect with his readers by putting some of the news in a personal context, entertaining them on occasion and making suggestions for community improvement and civic engagement. That said, Blackledge also was a realist:

> *Part of an editor's job is to offer opinions on how he thinks things ought to be done. If enough others agree with those opinions, sometimes a thing happens almost the way the editor wished. More often not. This editor has survived longer than most…by not being too surprised or disappointed when his advice is ignored—as it often is.*[250]

Blackledge began writing a personal column for the *Telegraph-Bulletin* in 1957 after he became the managing editor. Titled "Letter from the Editor: Your Town and Mine," the columns were published intermittently until 1959, when he left the paper to take a position at the *Miami Herald*. Topics varied. Sometimes he wrote about his young family. For example, when his sons Gene, age six, and Mark, four and a half, saw three whooping cranes resting near the Platte River during the annual spring migration—only thirty-two whoopers were in existence at that time—Blackledge wrote:

> [The boys] *became members at an early age of a rather select organization, the "I Saw a Whooping Crane Club." Their dad, who is considerably older, and has been chasing whooping crane rumors ever since he moved to our town over five years ago, also became a new member of the club yesterday.*[251]

Those initial columns consisted of the editor's thoughts on an assortment of subjects, including annual pancake feeds, United Fund drives, stories and tributes to hometown colleagues and friends and local political campaigns. On the day before the 1958 election, he urged readers to get out and vote, noting, "One political candidate faces trouble in about 14 years. His campaign pitch over TV interrupted *Popeye* and all the 7-year-olds on our block are against him for life."[252]

Blackledge's early columns revealed a dry wit the editor would continue to sharpen for years. Take this one about the spelling of the word for a candy made of brown sugar, cream and nuts. When society editor Marie Shannon "blew her top" over "pinucchi" in a *Telegraph-Bulletin* ad, the editor responded, "Looks all right to me. Isn't it some sort of candy?" The 1951 Webster's New Collegiate Sixth Edition only added to the confusion, with the editors finding "panocha" as the first spelling; however, also listed were "panoche," "panouchi," "penuche" and "penuchi." Commented Blackledge, "The editor still likes pinucchi."[253]

Early on, Blackledge frequently took pokes at bureaucrats and lawmakers. "Some of the best reading in the world is in the Nebraska Unicameral's *Legislative Journal*, a day-to-day-report of legislative happenings." He went on to point out the entry for the fifty-fifth day under "Corrections for the Journal," which read, "Page 937, line 27, delete the stricken comma after 'employees' and insert a stricken semicolon." Blackledge's rejoinder: "Now there's a sentence that requires a lot of thought. If you delete a comma that's stricken, does that mean the comma is back in? And is 'inserting' a 'stricken' semicolon the same as inserting no semicolon at all?"[254]

"Your Town and Mine" was published intermittently not long after Blackledge's return to the *Telegraph* as executive editor in 1967. The columns became a regular feature in the opinion pages on September 11, 1977, the day the *Telegraph* published its first weekend edition. According to Blackledge, "The column was intended to be a local-regional column of comment and observations more informally written, and more personal, than the regular *Telegraph* editorials."[255] Personal as in his annual birthday columns.

When Blackledge turned sixty-six, he shared with readers a birthday greeting he received from an old friend, who remembered the editor's thirty-fifth:

> *There was no question about it that you were the oldest person in the room. And you weren't much fun. You were convinced that, at 35, you were over the hill and senility couldn't be far behind. Really, the only fun time of the evening was when our beautiful collie puppy threw up on your shoe. All of us got such a kick out of that.*[256]

On his forty-seventh, Blackledge counseled:

> *Run hard now, young man, while running feels good. At 47 you will find it is no longer much pleasure, and have some regrets for the days you might have run, but only walked or sat instead....Love with intemperance. Work with passion. You will not regret later how much you did, or how generously you gave, but you may regret what you failed to do, or the gift you withheld.*[257]

When he turned sixty, he mused:

> *When you are 40, you note with some surprise that there seems to a good deal of life left. When you are 50, you scarcely notice. When you are 60, you begin to realize that people of 20, 30, 40 and even 50 think of you as old. What do they know? Life at 60 is full of contradictory emotions. You begin to wonder if you are getting the respect due your years. If you get some you are offended. That sort of respect ought to be reserved for older people.*[258]

And on his eightieth:

> *An old person is an old person. Why not admit it? I always ask for an old person's discount, which confuses young checkout people who have been led to believe "senior citizen" is the only politically correct way to refer to us.*[259]

Like the birthday columns, the editor annually shared his New Year's resolutions. Here's the list for 1985:

- *Write shorter editorials.*
- *Try to understand the problems of water resources, education, agriculture, banking, the economy and the Nebraska Legislature so I can write about them more intelligently.*
- *Read more poetry, less politics.*
- *Remember that Pointing with Pride and Viewing with Alarm can both be overdone.*
- *Write shorter columns.* [260]

Blackledge also provided tips for letters-to-the-editor writers:

> *The longest letter-to-the-editor on record was 13,000 words, written to the editor of the* Fishing Gazette *in 1884. It was published in small type in two issues of the magazine. Please try to keep your letters-to-the-editor of the* Telegraph *shorter than that. We do not seek to set a record.* [261]

In short, keep the letters short (his frequent advice), don't be cute and avoid sarcasm. Blackledge repeatedly reminded people that unsigned letters were never published. Such policies sometimes begat criticism:

> *Mr. Editor, I know you won't put this in the paper the way I wrote it, you're too afraid of freedom of speech in North Platte. You're too afraid you might step on somebody's toes. So throw it away like you do, or revise it so no one gets mad. I'm afraid also of retaliation so please don't use my name, or they'll all come down on me. Excuse the sloppiness I'm very angry.* [262]

To which the editor responded:

> *A few letters are edited. Not so "they wouldn't make anyone mad" but to eliminate phrases and allegations that would encourage a libel suit. And for that reason and others, some letters don't get printed at all. The letters column isn't a lost-and-found; it isn't another place to try a lawsuit, and it isn't a place to get even with your neighbor, your ex-spouse or someone who gave you a raw deal in business. You can't advocate violence or a boycott. We discourage, but don't rule out altogether, poetic letters....Excuse the sloppiness. I'm a little angry myself.* [263]

When the *Telegraph* changed its publishing schedule in 1979, Blackledge's columns brought readers in on the complex process involved in the transition from an afternoon to a morning paper. On the day the change was announced, he wrote:

> *Remember the* Daily Bulletin*? It was a morning newspaper in our town in the 1930s and early 1940s, and a lot of people liked it....A lot of things have changed in our town, and in towns throughout the area. We think those changes add up to sound reasons for making a change now. We are under no illusions that the changes will be universally applauded. Change never is.* [264]

But behind the scenes, Blackledge was not happy about the scheduling conversion. Although he understood that morning delivery had advantages for people and families squeezed for time, he liked the work routine associated with an afternoon paper. [265] Yet all the while, Blackledge reassured readers, "We think the result will be a better product, with more hours for preparation and delivery while you sleep, and more hours of useful life after it is delivered." [266]

Eric Seacrest, former Western Publishing chief executive officer and executive director of Mid-Nebraska Community Foundation, worked in the newsroom with Blackledge during the time of the scheduling change. He said that the transition was particularly challenging for the paper's editorial staff. [267] And when delivery routes were combined into fewer and larger routes, many carriers quit. On more than one occasion, Blackledge and Seacrest delivered the paper themselves.

Sometime during the switch, several "Ann Landers" columns didn't get published. "Nobody ever complains if the editorial is left out," complained Blackledge. "But someone always complains if *Ann Landers* is missing. Guess you know how that makes an editor feel. Maybe if I wrote to *Ann Landers*." [268]

After the change to morning delivery, the editorial operating cycle typically ended around 11:00 p.m. Still, Blackledge stuck to his routine of arriving at the paper early in the morning. While most reporters and editors departed before midnight, Blackledge never left the office until he had a copy of that day's paper in hand.

Eric Seacrest. *Eric Seacrest.*

He'd turn in shortly after getting home but often woke in the middle of the night to jot down an idea. Day or night, Blackledge was seldom seen without the yellow legal tablet on which he perpetually scribbled notes.[269]

A few years after the afternoon-to-morning scheduling change, *Telegraph* employees faced another challenge. Officially, moving day to the new building at 621 North Chestnut Street was February 22, 1981; nonetheless, for the next several weeks, the newspaper operated out of both new and old headquarters. During the first week in March, three press units were dissembled and moved into the new building, along with two additional units that were added to the system. Meanwhile, the *Telegraph* was printed on four units in the old building. Finally, all the units in the new building were ready to go, and on March 10, 1981, the first issue of the *Telegraph* in new quarters rolled off the presses. This completed the move from East Fifth Street, where the newspaper had operated since 1948.[270]

That spring, the *Telegraph* celebrated its 100th birthday with an open house with the U.S. Army Jazz Ambassadors performing the centennial birthday concert for more than 1,200 participants.[271] Blackledge and the news staff published a 100th anniversary special section that reproduced the front pages from the past century and the April 14, 1882 edition of the first *Telegraph*.

Before long, the former *Telegraph* building on East Fifth Street became the home of the Calvary Assembly of God Church. Pastor Ray Corlew took Blackledge's old office as his own. According to the editor:

> *I cut my journalism eyeteeth in that building in 50s and saw it through some grand and exciting times in the 70s. We turned out some good newspapers there, and worked with some wonderful people....Presently the old* Telegraph *is being cleaned of years of accumulated grease and ink mist and newsprint dust. It is getting new paint and new carpet. As Pastor Corlew showed where the pulpit and choir platform would be (about where several units of the press used to stand), I could begin to visualize it as a church. The upstairs balcony that was the newsroom several different times, and the lunch room and conference room, finally, will be Sunday school classrooms. The level of discussion will be much improved, I feel sure.*[272]

Blackledge's columns occasionally drew on extraordinary happenings in North Platte. Like the "Great Grape Controversy," as it came to be known, which occurred in the summer of 1981. After a young Frenchwoman, off a tour bus stop in North Platte, took a single grape from a bunch at a local grocery store, she was hauled off to jail and charged with shoplifting.[273] The charge soon was dismissed and the fifty-dollar bond refunded, but the story made the wire services anyway. Thanks to a number of North Platte–area people, who wrote to her expressing regret, Veronique Talpe forgave the city. A "Your Town and Mine" column included a letter from Talpe to a local woman, which said in part:

> *It is true that I had a poor idea of your city after I left it, and it is true also that all the signs of friendship I received at home make me feel much better about it....Please would you mind inserting a word in your paper to thank everyone....I would also like you to know that an American man—the bus driver—helped me for paying the fine. I am reimbursing him....So now I can think about the friendship of a city and about the generosity of a bus driver with a vanishing souvenir of the bad event.* [274]

Blackledge noted that "a major international misunderstanding has been avoided." He added, "Credit the spontaneous personal involvement of a number of people from our town and area." [275] Talpe, a nurse, later traveled to India to help in the treatment of people with leprosy.

On August 13, 1987, President Ronald Reagan came to town. Following a barbecue at a local ranch, Reagan spoke in the early afternoon before a crowd estimated at fifteen thousand at the NEBRASKAland Days Wild West Arena. The president praised the North Platte Canteen, which he said exemplified "the spirit of this great country of ours, independent and full of heart." [276] Blackledge said it was the first presidential visit to North Platte since 1948 and a gift to the city from Governor Kay Orr, who "nagged the White House to get the President to a Nebraska stopover outside of Lincoln or Omaha." [277]

President Reagan made three visits to North Platte. In addition to the one in 1987, he stopped while on the presidential primary campaign trail in 1976, and he made a return post-presidential visit in 1990 when he flew to North Platte to lend a campaign hand to Governor Orr.

On Reagan's last visit, Blackledge observed:

> *Love him or hate him—he was President of this nation for eight years. As can be said of any presidency, some good things and some bad things happened in that time....At any rate, he is undeniably a historic figure. And he comes to North Platte today as the only President to have visited our town before he was President, while he was President, and after he was President. For an "isolated town" (as we were described in the* Wall Street Journal *recently) that in itself is something.* [278]

Blackledge was proud of the fact that stage, film and television star Jane Alexander had a connection to North Platte. He liked to remind readers that the actress, a Massachusetts native, was the granddaughter of Dr. Daniel T. Quigley, a pioneer in the use of radium in the treatment of cancer; he was also Buffalo Bill Cody's family physician in North Platte from 1906 to 1914.[279] In 1991, Blackledge nominated Alexander for the NEBRASKAland Days Buffalo Bill Award.

But the Buffalo Bill Award that year went to Alex Cord because, according to the NEBRASKAland Days Board, the actor was better known to the younger generation. Cord played the character Archangel in the television action series *Airwolf*, which ran from 1984 to 1986 on CBS and for a time in 1987 on USA Network. Blackledge wasn't happy:

> *Apparently she* [Jane Alexander] *wasn't considered current enough or famous enough, though she was then starring in a Broadway play and had won an Emmy nomination and a Western Heritage award some years earlier for her role in the CBS production of* Calamity Jane.[280]

In 1993, President Bill Clinton appointed Alexander chair of the National Endowment for the Arts, a position she held until 1997, when she returned to acting.

The fact that the *Telegraph* had its own political cartoonist for a time was extraordinary too. The *Bieber Cartoon* was a regular Saturday feature on the opinion pages from 1970 to 1976. "The *Telegraph* may be the smallest daily newspaper featuring its own editorial cartoonist. Certainly we are the smallest represented in *Best Editorial Cartoons of the Year, 1976*," Blackledge said.[281] The cartoonist, Carl Bieber, a rural mail carrier, often lampooned city and county officials as well as state and national figures. Bieber served as mayor of North Platte from 1976 to 1980. In his editorial endorsing candidate Bieber, Blackledge commented:

> *If Bieber gets elected mayor, it will be in spite of, not because of his cartoons. A cartoonist is sure to ruffle someone's feathers with almost every piece he publishes. Over a period of time, the law of averages dictates that he will have angered almost everyone at one time or another. It is the same way with editorial writers....If the cartoonist or editorial writer manages to retain a few friends in spite of this, it is a considerable tribute to the generosity and open-mindedness of those friends.*[282]

Blackledge also valued the contributions of John Martinez, veteran *Telegraph* sports editor, who joined the staff in 1966. But Martinez was more than the sports editor. Blackledge referred to him as "a sort of news staff social director." He explained:

> *The group that met for last call after the paper was finished for that night called themselves the "Understaff." Understaff "meetings" helped rookies and veterans blow off the steam of frustration at stories missed because someone didn't call, or because of computer glitches. They calmed nerves strung out from frantic efforts to find the right words for too much information in too little time. They helped pass along the history and culture of this particular newsroom. This was where young reporters fresh out of college learned how things really worked and gained a feeling for the traditions of this newspaper and this community.*[283]

He added, "John didn't rule the Understaff, of course. Part of the characteristic of an understaff is there can be no ruler. John was the godfather, the humorist-historian, the caller of the meetings."[284]

Following Martinez's death on July 6, 1991, Blackledge wrote:

> *[T]he kind of thing John brought to this paper happens or it doesn't. When it happens you have a group of people working not for the "Boss"…but for each other and for the tradition that binds them together.*[285]

Meanwhile, Blackledge established traditions of his own. His distinctive voice when speaking to readers imbued the opinion pages of the paper for years, and his acumen in the newsroom left an indelible mark on many of the young journalists who worked there. As one former reporter recounted:

> *I learned more at North Platte than anywhere before or since.…I have more or less maintained a career in journalism since working at the* Telegraph. *But I've never sensed the same depth of feeling about my job—the feeling that I was making a contribution; the gratification when the paper was good, the anger/fear/regret when things didn't go well.*[286]

Such sentiment goes far toward explaining how the *Telegraph* became family for many and a place budding news people fondly remembered for years to come.

Chapter 7

THE EDITOR AND MENTOR

For many, this was their first full-time newspaper job. Some of them came with
journalism degrees from excellent colleges or universities. But it is true in this
business, as in many others, that the classroom can only do so much. You are not
a newspaper person until you have done some postgraduate education in real life.
We do not give degrees, but we are a graduate school of journalism nevertheless.
Among the instructors are our readers and our news sources. Nothing drives home
a lesson about accuracy and responsibility more forcefully than an irate subscriber
who has caught a reporter or editor in a careless mistake. This is a school in
which the lessons and lectures never end.
—Keith Blackledge[287]

Although not a schoolroom, the *North Platte Telegraph* newsroom
nonetheless became a place where Keith Blackledge helped young
reporters and editors find their own voices and grow as journalists and
individuals. In 1968, one year after Blackledge returned to the *Telegraph*
as the new executive editor, Jo Ann became the journalism teacher at
North Platte High School. Thus, nearly twenty years after the Blackledges
graduated with journalism degrees from the University of Missouri—the
country's oldest and, according to some, finest college of journalism—they
both were working with young people learning the couple's beloved craft.
It's not hard to imagine the suppertime conversations back then concerning
misspellings, grammatical errors, awkward sentences, buried ledes, statter
quotes, story holes…and then chuckles, headshakes, shared words of hope
and pride when one of their charges showed promise.

Many of the people who did the work of journalism with Blackledge at the *Telegraph* describe him as their editor-mentor. At five-foot-seven and slight of build, Blackledge was hardly a physically imposing man. Yet whenever the editor stood outside his office door, or while taking one of his fabled strolls through the newsroom, the staff was well aware of his larger-than-life presence. According to Dan Moser, who joined the *Telegraph* as a general news reporter in 1983, stories abounded for years among former reporters, editors and photographers about how terrified they all had been of Blackledge.[288] The editor's taciturn nature augmented his formidability. As Moser noted, "He was a guy who used silence to great effect."[289]

David Anderson, who worked at the *Telegraph-Bulletin* in 1958, dubbed Blackledge's signature sign of disapproval the "Baleful Glare." He explained:

> *Keith could hold that look longer than I ever saw anyone hold that look. Head up, motionless, pencil poised as if to write, staring across the newsroom. Would he smash the pencil? Shout? No. After about half a lifetime, head thrown back, sniffing disdainfully and turning his back, he'd strip the wire.*[290]

Anderson considers himself one of Blackledge's earliest projects. The Harvard University freshman from Gothenburg, Nebraska, was taking a year off from school when he walked into the newsroom looking for a job. Blackledge, the paper's managing editor at the time, remembered the young Anderson: "He didn't know how to type, but I figured anyone with a four-year scholarship to Harvard was smart enough to learn quickly."[291]

Anderson said that Blackledge's guidance took the form of reticence... and probes:

> *Keith didn't critique our stories so much as he asked questions that made us critique them ourselves. If we quoted a council member, Keith might ask, "Did he say this in reference to the budget?" Whatever our answer, Keith would often just continue looking at the story in silence. Those long silences were among his most effective tool. While we were waiting for him to say something more, we would ask ourselves a hundred questions: Did the quote really capture what the guy meant? Did he say something more that ought to be included? Could we have misunderstood him? Should we have asked him to clarify? Keith might say nothing more, but he usually didn't need to.*[292]

After the *Telegraph-Bulletin*, Anderson graduated from Harvard.[293] He was working for United Press International when Blackledge recruited him as financial editor of the *Dayton (OH) Journal-Herald*, where Blackledge was then assistant managing editor. Neither man stayed in Dayton. In 1967, Blackledge returned to Nebraska, while Anderson went on to earn a law degree from the University of Texas School of Law, where in 1971 he joined the faculty. Blackledge eventually would help Anderson research his memoir about growing up in rural Lincoln County. "Just as crucially, Keith encouraged and prodded me to finish the book during the 25 years I took to write it."[294]

According to Anderson, "Keith had a genius for giving a young reporter the right mix of guidance, responsibility, and freedom....He became famous for hiring kids like me and turning us into reporters."[295]

Sharron Hollen, another early Blackledge protégé, began her newspaper career at the *Telegraph-Bulletin* in 1960. "Every reporter will say that Keith was a phenomenal teacher—and task master. There was just something about him that made reporters want to do their very best."[296] She added:

> *Keith didn't hang over a person's shoulder, or go over every story with a reporter line by line, before or after publication. But on some stories, he would ask, "Is this the most important thing you had to say?" And then he'd go back to editing the story and leave you sitting there in the silence. Well, was that the most important thing or is there anything different I should do with this story? And he didn't expect an answer. He expected action.*[297]

Sometime later, after the birth of Hollen's daughter and during her two-week maternity leave, she got a phone call from Blackledge:

> *Keith said, "I need you to do just this one story; bring her to work; we can fix up a desk drawer for her. I'll help take care of her." So it became an almost daily thing. "Well, I need this story, or I need that story," he would say. And so my daughter lived in a desk drawer, and Keith helped tend to her. So babysitting was part of what he did well also. And he had a way with kids. He* did *have a way with kids.*[298]

Judy Nelson, the *Telegraph's* farm editor from 1972 to 1975, said that Blackledge was "a great teacher, not because he said I am going to teach you, but by the way he practiced journalism."[299] Nelson added that Blackledge also taught by parable.[300] Whenever things got quiet in the newsroom or when people were sitting around a table at the White Horse after putting the paper to bed, every so often the editor would tell a story. "No Photos of Elephants" was one of his favorites. Nelson's too:

> *While at the newspaper in Miami, Keith said the word from on high was to never publish photos of elephants on the front page. No one knew the reason for the edict—pictures of elephants likely had been overdone in the past— but they knew enough not to ask questions and follow the rules. One day, a bona fide elephant stampede occurred somewhere in the vicinity—the details of the stampede by now have been forgotten.* The New York Times *published a photo of the stampede on its front page, along with many other newspapers across the nation. The* Miami Herald, *however, did not.*[301]

One day, Blackledge asked Nelson to write a weekly column. As Blackledge explained the column's genesis:

> *Judy would occasionally write me notes about her work, observations on human nature, touches of philosophy, or flights of fancy prompted by the season.....I decided those notes were worth sharing with readers. I edited one a little, put a headline on it, and ran it as a personal column under the heading* Poor Judy's Almanac.[302]

Nelson complied with the editor's request "with trepidation," and "Poor Judy's Almanac" was published for the next twenty years.

Whenever inexperienced reporters joined the news staff, Blackledge started them out by writing deaths and weather—to their dismay. Several remembered exactly what the editor had to say to them at the time. "Everybody talks about one, and does the other, and only a good reporter can write it well," former staffers remember Blackledge saying.

According to Hollen, if mistakes got made—as invariably could happen with a young staff—there was likely to be "some hell to pay." She added, "You were allowed mistakes, but never the same one twice."[303]

Yet Blackledge also was his reporters' biggest defender. They were confident that the editor would stand behind them in public, and while he might take them apart in private, they knew he always would have their backs.[304]

Dan Moser provided one such example. During the Nebraska primary race for the Republican nomination for U.S. Senate in 1984, Moser interviewed State Senator John DeCamp[305] during one of the candidate's many campaign stops in newsrooms across the state. Concerning opponent

Nancy Hoch,[306] the only woman among all six contenders for the seat, DeCamp remarked, "Nancy's a good looking broad, but she's shallow on the issues."[307] After the story was published—the ill-fated statement included—an outraged DeCamp at first denied saying it. Then he said the reporter overhead him saying it to someone else, and then he tried to wiggle out of it because he said the word *broad* has numerous meanings.[308]

Failing to get the paper to retract, DeCamp barged in on Blackledge at his home, demanding that "that chicken shit reporter be fired." Hours later, the disappointed DeCamp stormed out. The next day, Blackledge stopped by Moser's desk and said, "If you ever again cause DeCamp to come to my house on a Sunday afternoon for three hours, I may have to consider firing you."[309] When Moser was named managing editor of the *Telegraph* in 1990, Blackledge said, "Moser may be the best all-around reporter of my experience."[310]

David Anderson, who eventually became the cops and courts reporter during his stint at the paper in 1958, said that he had Blackledge's unwavering support when the parents of six high school football players, accused of a gang rape, complained that Anderson's coverage of the trial was unfair to their sons. "Blackledge asked me to explain my reporting to him, and then he faced the parents and backed me up."[311] Anderson later recalled:

> *I realize that it was a demonstration of quiet courage on his part—the courage to trust his reporters and to believe that in the long run giving us our heads would produce a better paper and a better community.... Undoubtedly we caused him some grief with his friends and readers, but he didn't clip our wings. He gave us responsibility, and at the same time made us take responsibility for what we did.*[312]

In 1968, Mary Ann Koch took a part-time job in the *Telegraph's* composing room; she later moved to the accounting department. Aware of her high school newspaper and yearbook experience, Blackledge asked her to do a story for the cover of the weekend tabloid edition about her hometown of Gandy, Nebraska. Readers liked the story, as did Blackledge, and Koch continued to freelance feature stories until joining the news staff full time in 1970. She became the family page editor in 1971 and the regional editor for the newspaper's twenty-two-county area in west-central Nebraska in 1980. For many years, she also wrote a personal column titled "Dear People."

Blackledge and Koch became friends, as did the two families. Years later, Blackledge described the friendships:

> *They went to the same church. Soon they were sharing meals as families and occasionally going out as couples to dances or other social events. The two husbands got along well, and so did the two wives. The five boys (his three, her two) matched up well.*[313]

Meanwhile, the bond deepened between Koch and Blackledge. He recalled:

> *The editor needed someone to talk to as a friend, not a boss. With all gender barriers now suspect, no reason his friend could not be a woman. They began sharing a lunch hour now and then, or a drive in the park. Just talking. She was his sounding board....Just business or idle conversation or sharing history and viewpoints.*[314]

The friendship grew into love. And although Blackledge, Jo Ann and Mary Ann would remain friends, these were difficult times. Former new staff people said they were mostly surprised that the two seemed to think that no one knew about their relationship.

The couples divorced. Blackledge and Mary Ann were married in 1994. When Jo Ann Blackledge[315] died on April 23, 2007, Blackledge and Mary Ann were at her bedside. In a tribute to his former wife, Blackledge wrote:

> *If you add one bit of knowledge, understanding and appreciation to a youngster's life at the right time, it stays with that person 60, 70, perhaps 80 years....Jo Ann Blackledge did that in high school journalism classes, giving students the elements of good writing, honest reporting and ethical standards. These are good things to have in your background whether you become a journalist or not.*[316]

In the meantime, life went on at the newspaper. The staff was interested in learning newspapering from Blackledge, and Blackledge resolved to teach them. George Hipple,[317] who was the news photographer at the *Telegraph* from 1984 to 1995, said:

> *Keith inspired us to do better than we could ever imagine. He wanted all of us to become the best, not just as journalists or photojournalists, but as contributing members of society. We are better because of him....I'm one of the lucky ones to have had Keith as somebody in my life; he made me who I am today.*[318]

Blackledge hired Peggy Woodruff as Hipple's assistant in 1988, despite her lack of news photography experience. Woodruff said that she considered it an honor and a privilege to work in the *Telegraph* newsroom. In her three and a half years there, she said she never once saw Blackledge get angry. "He just handled everything and things seemed to flow over him," she commented. "He was so gentle and so kind."[319]

Mary Hepburn said she's another person Blackledge took a chance on. In 1968, Blackledge put the recent high school graduate to work part time on the news staff during the school year so she could attend junior college classes and full time during summers. Hepburn went on to get a degree in education and journalism from the University of Nebraska–Lincoln. She remembered Blackledge with great affection:

> *Keith stuck with me. I learned a lot and I owe my desire to want to be a journalist to him. I don't think Keith ever realized how many people he affected and inspired to be what they have become.*[320]

Hepburn[321] returned the *Telegraph* in 1996, whereupon Blackledge told readers, "It's good to have Mary back….She added something special to our paper when she was 18, and she is adding something special again."[322] Today, Hepburn continues to write the column "Church News and Views" for the *Telegraph*.

Rodney Wenz[323] covered sports part time as a high school student in 1953, when Blackledge was sports editor of the *Telegraph-Bulletin*. Afterward, Blackledge followed Wenz's flourishing journalism career, and some fifty-five years later, he successfully nominated Wenz for a North Platte High School distinguished alumni award. Wenz, who studied journalism at the University of Nebraska–Lincoln and the University of Kentucky, became an investigative reporter, a bureau chief and business editor in Illinois and Kentucky. He later launched a public relations firm in Louisville, Kentucky. Wenz spoke fondly of North Platte, including his time at the paper with Blackledge, whom he said he considered one of the greatest mentors of his life.[324]

Jill Claflin began her journalism career at the *Telegraph* in 1980 as a weekend copy editor.[325] After stints at the *Cincinnati (OH) Post* and co-ownership the *Callaway Courier*, she returned to the *Telegraph* in 1985 as the new managing editor. Claflin observed that "Keith would cultivate the people he hired. He would figure out what motivated them, and how to speak to them as individuals. He was so insightful, and so quiet that it didn't always show."[326]

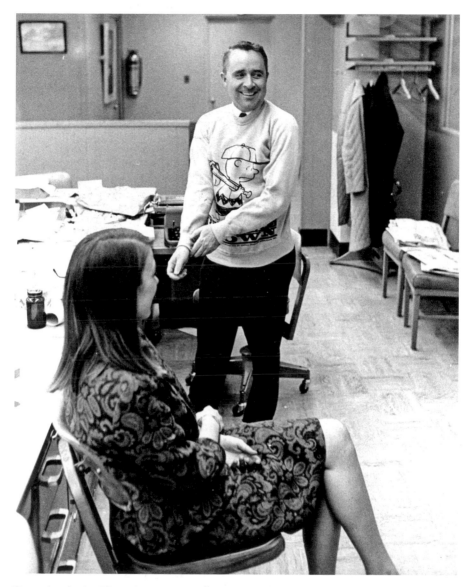

Downtime in the *Telegraph* newsroomn as Blackledge has some fun with a young news staffer. Role playing was a favorite game. *Blackledge Collection*.

Life outside the newsroom included social gatherings, Super Bowl parties and Sunday afternoon get-togethers with families and friends. And more than one talked about the sense of community in the newsroom—an atmosphere they said Blackledge created. Reunions among the former news team and the Blackledges were common throughout the years. When Blackledge was inducted into the University of Nebraska Newspaper Hall of Fame on October 7, 2005, many of the staff came back to Nebraska to honor their former editor. Numerous former *Telegraph* news people remained family to the Blackledges long after his retirement.

Besides lessons in the newsroom, Blackledge's colleagues and friends also said they learned from the editor. Former Nebraska secretary of state John Gale, whose political beginnings were in Lincoln County, sought Blackledge's guidance before he successfully was elected chairman of the Nebraska State Republican Party in 1985.[327]

Former Nebraska secretary of state John Gale. *John Gale.*

Blackledge later encouraged Gale when he considered a run for a seat in U.S. House of Representatives after Nebraska's Third District congressman, Bill Barrett, announced his retirement. The editor helped Gale establish a campaign committee and spearheaded the fundraising. In November 1999, Gale declared himself a GOP Congressional candidate. "Keith was willing to help people who were willing to stretch themselves."[328]

Gale said that he visited every town in every district in Nebraska, while the campaign raised the $100,000 needed to get it off the ground. Among the five other Republican candidates, Gale was the frontrunner. "It was so much fun," he recounted—that is, until former Nebraska Huskers football coach and state luminary Tom Osborne jumped in.[329] Gale said he learned of Osborne's candidacy while he was driving to a fundraiser in Grand Island. He abruptly canceled the event, as well as a stop scheduled in Omaha the next day, at which point Blackledge offered, "John, you are in this race because you are well-intentioned, and you will be good for Nebraska. You were never guaranteed a victory so let's stay in and stick to the issues and see what happens." Osborne handily won the seat, but Gale remains proud that he carried his own Lincoln County, although he got clobbered everywhere else. "I took a big financial hit, but I loved running for the office."[330]

When Gale was offered the Nebraska secretary of state position in 2000, he again sought Blackledge's guidance. Blackledge told him that the appointment was better than a Congressional seat anyway. "Keith was right," commented Gale, who said the position was the capstone of his career.[331] Gale retired in 2018.

Gary Toebben, former president of the North Platte Chamber of Commerce, referred to Blackledge as his friend, cohort, mentor and surrogate father.[332] Toebben—who went on to head chambers in Kansas, Kentucky and California—had a favorite Blackledge story:

> *While Keith was a great writer, he would never write out his speeches in advance. I am just the opposite, so his lack of preparation caused me alarm. During the meal prior to his speech, Keith would start making notes on a paper napkin and when it was his turn, those notes became the core of his speech. When he finished, I would smile and applaud with envy, until the next time when I again would feel the same level of anxiety. Whether from his manual typewriter or notes from a napkin, Keith Blackledge was the best, and he taught me more about community development than any other mentor in my 39 years of chamber work.*[333]

Former *Chicago Tribune* newspaperman Bob Greene and Blackledge became friends during the time the editor helped Greene research his book *Once Upon a Town*, about the North Platte World War II Canteen, published in 2002. But the friendship would come years after Blackledge had to explain to Greene a few things about hunting in Nebraska.

At the height of the 1980 hunting season, Greene, in his syndicated column "Ringside Reporter," characterized hunters as the "sickest of America's sick." He also speculated that hunting must be "satisfying some need to watch things die."[334] Besieged by calls from angry readers, Blackledge wrote in an editorial titled "A Letter from the Editor to Bob Greene":

> *I'd already tried explaining to several callers that I don't agree with everything that goes on our opinion page. They surely, I argued, wouldn't want an opinion page that reflected only one point of view. That would eliminate a lot of letters to the editor, for one thing, and quite a few syndicated columns and cartoons.....None of these arguments seemed very convincing to the people I was talking to. Come to think of it, they didn't seem very convincing to me.*[335]

Blackledge went on to write about the times he'd hunted with his father, his sons and his friends. The beauty of cold snowy sunrises. The occasional wild duck dinner shared among family and friends during fall. With that, he closed:

Your hunting column was junk, Bob. I'm sorry that I gave it space in my paper. I'm sorry not only for the hunters I've offended, but for the non-hunters who, not knowing any differently, may choose to adopt your prejudice as their own. Sincerely, Keith Blackledge, Editor.[336]

In the next "Ringside Reporter" column, Greene praised Blackledge for publishing the disagreeable column:

What is heartening to me is how seriously editors take their responsibilities of providing a good product for their readers. In North Platte, Nebraska, Keith Blackledge, editor of the Telegraph, *hated the column. He is a hunter, and he thought I was dead wrong. But he felt that his opinion page shouldn't be limited to his own opinions, and he ran it anyway.*[337]

Later, during Greene's time in North Platte while working on his book about the canteen, Greene said that his respect for Blackledge grew. Did the two ever discuss the offensive column? Said Greene:

Yes, he and I did talk—and laugh—about it. Keith was always meticulous in his reasoning. It was hard to argue with the conclusions in a Keith Blackledge column. If Keith thought I had missed the mark on something, then I had probably missed the mark. I appreciated his constructive criticism as much as I did his praise.[338]

In the acknowledgements page of his book, Greene commended the editor: "If every newspaperman and newspaperwoman approached the job in the clear-eyed and honest way that Mr. Blackledge does...then we would never have to worry about the public having a low opinion of our business."[339]

Columnist and author Bob Greene. *Bob Greene.*

Indeed, from the time Blackledge returned to the *Telegraph* in 1967 until his retirement in 1992, he diligently worked to provide readers with quality local and regional news. And in so doing, he gained a reputation for hiring and helping talented young people learn the trade.

In August 1976, Jeff Funk arrived at the *Telegraph* as the new courts reporter. But before long, the courthouse beat was in trouble, and Blackledge—while coaching the brash young reporter—became locked in a years-long battle with an antagonistic Lincoln County district judge.

Chapter 8

NEBRASKA PRESS ASSOCIATION V. STUART

The Crime, the Conflict and the Aftermath

The press of Nebraska disputes that [the judge] *had no choice but to restrict the press in order to do his duty in protecting the defendant's right to a fair trial. The reader may wonder why. Many preliminary hearings are not covered in detail. In many others the press voluntarily refrains from reporting segments which would be prejudicial, sometimes of its own volition and sometimes at the request of judges or attorneys. But when any court lays down a rule that…may have the effect of law, the press has an obligation to oppose such restriction.*
—*Keith Blackledge*[340]

The U.S. Supreme Court ruling in *Nebraska Press Association v. Stuart* on June 30, 1976, ended the free press/fair trial conflict originating with the *North Platte Telegraph* over its coverage of a murderer's criminal prosecution. The decision: the lower courts' efforts to gag the press were unconstitutional under the First Amendment.

The conflict preceding the high court decision had its beginning with a heinous crime and the capture of a killer. The subsequent attempts by the Lincoln County courts to restrict the news coverage landed the *North Platte Telegraph* and its editor, Keith Blackledge, in a legal battleground that eventually drew the nation's attention.

At odds were two highly cherished constitutional protections: the First Amendment's guarantee that the press has a right to publish—the implication of which is to protect the public's right to timely news—and the Sixth Amendment's guarantee that a criminal defendant has the right to a fair and public trial before an impartial jury.

In North Platte, the time preceding the Supreme Court decision was filled with the intense effort of battling the issue in courtrooms and on street corners while *Telegraph* editors and reporters—under trying and emotional circumstances—continued to gather and write the news.

It began on Saturday evening, October 18, 1975, when *North Platte Telegraph* assistant editor Bill Eddy returned home after covering the Nebraska Jaycees convention and received a phone call. A gunman was on the loose in North Platte! Eddy soon learned that a family—including children—had been murdered in Sutherland, Nebraska, a town of about 850 people some twenty-five miles west of North Platte.[341] The killer had not been apprehended. Heading to the *Telegraph* office, Eddy made a quick stop at Blackledge's home to alert his editor, already in bed, that something big was going on. The editor's wife, Jo Ann, went to rouse her husband, while Eddy thought out the news coverage. Within moments, the sleepy editor listened as Eddy related what details about the crime he'd already been able to gather. Blackledge told Eddy "to take care of it," whereupon Eddy summoned about a half-dozen *Telegraph* news staffers, sending several to Sutherland, one to the North Platte hospital and the rest to the *Telegraph* office to make and take phone calls.[342]

The story was beginning to unfold. Earlier that day, twenty-nine-year-old Erwin Charles Simants watched neighbor ten-year-old Florence Kellie play in the yard of her Sutherland home, across the street from where Simants lived with relatives. Simants retrieved a .22-caliber rifle, loaded it with shells and made his way to the Kellies' small white frame house.[343]

Florence, who had gone inside by then, let Simants in. After first attempting to sexually assault the girl, Simants shot her in the right temple at point-blank range, after which he continued the sexual assault. Then the killing spree began as Kellie family members separately returned home.[344] The victims:

- Florence Kellie, a fifth grader at Sutherland Elementary School. Audrey Marie Kellie and her husband, Henry, were legal guardians of their granddaughter after Florence's mother, Jennie, was killed in an auto accident in 1966.
- Henry Kellie, sixty-six, a semiretired farm laborer.
- Audrey Marie Kellie, fifty-seven, Henry's wife and a cook at the Sutherland Moore Memorial Nursing Home.
- David Kellie, thirty-two, the Kellies' only son. He lived near his parents and worked at a grain mill in Hershey, Nebraska.

- Deanna Kellie, seven, David's daughter.
- Daniel Kellie, five, David's son.

The females were sexually molested postmortem. The rampage lasted less than forty-five minutes, after which Simants returned home and unloaded and put away the gun. Sitting at the kitchen table, he scribbled out a note: "I am sorry to all it is the Best way out DO NOT crie [*sic*]."[345] This would be the first of several so-called confessions he would make. Simants then went to his parents' Sutherland home and described the crime. Simants's disbelieving father, Amos, rushed to the Kellie house, where he discovered the carnage. He summoned an ambulance and told his son to turn himself in. Instead, Simants fled.[346]

Soon the scene outside the Kellie home was abuzz with the activities of rescue squad workers and members of various law enforcement agencies, while news reporters and other onlookers also sought access. A Denver NBC television affiliate's chartered helicopter hovered over the house even before the bodies had been removed.[347]

As the manhunt for Simants continued, news organizations from across the nation were calling law enforcement, city hall and the newspaper for information. Eddy said that the *Telegraph* was swamped with phone calls throughout the night, including one from the BBC. While stories were being transmitted to the Associated Press wire service, Eddy was on the phone with editors and reporters from Nebraska newspapers and broadcast outlets. The news staff worked throughout the night. Blackledge checked in sometime before dawn.[348]

After Simants fled his parents' home, he walked to Sutherland's Rodeo Bar, where he'd been drinking heavily earlier that day. He downed one beer and then sauntered down the street to the town's other bar, the Longhorn, where he downed two more beers and left. That night, he hid in the weeds in the backyards and fields on the outskirts of town. He was apprehended early Sunday morning. Later that morning, he was arraigned before Lincoln County court judge Ronald Ruff, who set the preliminary hearing for Wednesday, October 22, at 9:00 a.m.[349]

The months-long legal skirmish was about to begin. Because of the timing of Saturday night's crime, radio and television coverage was ahead of the newspapers. Thus, Simants already had been apprehended and arraigned before the *Telegraph*'s initial coverage. The front page in Monday's paper was almost entirely devoted to the murders, with photos of Simants and the victims—including the fact that Simants had admitted to the crimes.

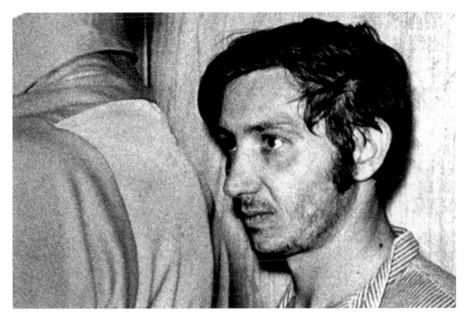

Erwin Charles Simants. *From the* North Platte Telegraph.

The publication of the so-called confessions would become key in the legal conflict that followed. There were four in total: the note he scrawled out immediately following the murder spree, two separate verbal confessions to family and an oral statement Simants gave to law enforcement following his apprehension.[350]

State and national news stories generally portrayed Simants as having low intelligence, as well as being semiliterate, often jobless, a drinker and a troublemaker.[351]

Both the prosecution and defense and the county judge were facing a constitutional crisis: how to safeguard the trial of a loathsome man who had committed appalling crimes. Certainly, Simants's personal deficiencies were well known in the community. Moreover, attorneys felt it vital to keep from the public the shocking nature of the crimes—child rape and necrophilia—which would become evident during the preliminary hearing when the first evidence against the defendant would be presented. Accordingly, the prosecution requested that Judge Ruff issue a gag order limiting the information the press could make public.[352]

By late Tuesday afternoon, the day before the preliminary hearing, the young and relatively inexperienced Judge Ruff and his staff had phoned local media, inviting them to the courthouse at 7:30 p.m. that evening. Ruff told Blackledge that he wanted to discuss the limitations on news coverage he would implement at the next morning's preliminary hearing.[353]

Those phone calls from the Lincoln County Court set off the alarm bells. Phone lines buzzed across the state as a response to the county judge was strategized. The first order of business: secure legal representation for the court session, scheduled only a few hours away.[354] *Telegraph* owner Joe R. Seacrest of Lincoln-Star Publishing got immediately to work. But the logistics proved daunting. It would take hours to drive the distance from Omaha or Lincoln to the courthouse in North Platte. Moreover, the company's regular First Amendment lawyers weren't available. Finally, late in the afternoon, *Telegraph* publisher Jim Seacrest asked North Platte attorney Harold Kay[355] to represent the media at the courthouse that evening.[356]

When Kay arrived, he found a gaggle of reporters waiting in the hall outside the locked courtroom. Among them was associate editor Eddy. Blackledge had opted instead to celebrate the passage of a long-fought school bond issue that evening. "Keith just had so much confidence that we would get the job done—and we did," commented Eddy.[357]

After pounding on the door to no avail, Kay finally located the court clerk and demanded entry.[358] Bursting in, he beheld an informal gathering of

North Platte attorney Harold Kay. *Stephen W. Kay.*

lawyers in Judge Ruff's office. Later in the courtroom, Ruff took the bench and listened as Kay argued that restricting the press in the open preliminary hearing would be unconstitutional under the First Amendment. Kay also asked that the media be given adequate time to prepare a legal response should such an order be rendered. Kay further contended that it was a violation of the state's open meetings laws to proceed that evening without a court reporter.[359] Kay referred to the gathering as a star chamber.[360]

The next morning, at Simants's preliminary hearing, Judge Ruff read the decree: no one involved in the case and present at the hearing will disseminate any testimony or evidence presented; the news media will adhere to the Nebraska Bar–Press Guidelines when determining what information to publish. That Ruff's order incorporated the guidelines infuriated media organizations, and it became for many the most egregious aspect of the entire controversy.[361]

The Bar-Press Guidelines was the byproduct after representatives of the Nebraska bar and news media sat down in 1970 to devise a plan to balance the conflicting rights of free press and fair trial. The document provided guidance to the media about the kinds of information deemed suitable for publication in criminal prosecutions. The guidelines were established as purely voluntary. As Blackledge vowed in an editorial following Ruff's order, "We will not enter again soon into any so-called 'voluntary' codes."[362]

Information considered inappropriate for publication includes the existence of information about confessions or statements, admissions of guilt and third-party opinions expressed about the guilt or innocence of the accused. Also frowned on is the dissemination of information relating to the accused's criminal background.

Because of Nebraska statutes at the time, Ruff was unable to close the preliminary hearing, which the media argued weakened any justification for the gag order. Anyone attending the preliminary hearing would hear the grisly details of the crime. What was to stop them from sharing the particulars with friends and neighbors?

The procedural path and jurisdictional complexities of this case are outside the scope of this book. In brief, a total of four gag orders would be issued before the case reached the U.S. Supreme Court. Lincoln County judge Ruff issued the first. Within a week, Lincoln County district judge Hugh Stuart considered the media's appeal and extended the gag with minor revisions. Later, an Eighth Circuit Court of Appeals chamber decision left intact portions of the gag. The Nebraska Supreme Court issued the final order restraining the press.

Nebraska entities joining the litigation included executives and leaders of Nebraska's Associated Press bureau in Omaha, the *Omaha World-Herald*, the *Lincoln Journal*, the Nebraska Press Association, the Nebraska Broadcasters Association, Sigma Delta Chi of Nebraska (a fraternal organization for professional journalists) and Media of Nebraska.[363]

One day, following the first order to muzzle his newspaper, Blackledge declared, "A subservient right is no right at all!" referring to the county judge's conclusion that the press must be subservient to rights of due process.[364] In the editorial, Blackledge chastised the lawyers for their loss of faith in the jury system and for doubting the effectiveness of remedies available to judges to counter the potential for jury bias.

The second gag order against the press was entered during another rare night court session before Lincoln County district judge Stuart on Thursday, October 23. Kay, joined now by Omaha attorney Stephen McGill, argued against the press restrictions. At some point during the hearing, McGill declared, "I'd let somebody go free who was guilty before I'd deny freedom of speech."[365] That widely publicized statement angered Judge Stuart, who extended the restrictive order. It also fueled the anti-press sentiment that had already begun to percolate in and around North Platte.[366]

Stuart's decision would become the focal point of all subsequent litigation in the appellate courts—forever linking his name to one of the foremost First Amendment U.S. Supreme Court decisions in history.

In a 2014 interview, former *Telegraph* publisher Seacrest became emotional when he described the vital role Harold Kay had played. Indeed, the argument Kay advanced in Stuart's courtroom on behalf of the media eventually would be the heart of the arguments presented later by other distinguished lawyers before the highest court in the land.[367] Kay had maintained: absolutely no evidence of inappropriate news reporting had been established; the Bar-Press Guidelines should function without judicial interference; and the court should never engage in the kind of prior restraint fundamental in the gag order.[368]

The *Telegraph* news staff covered the crime and the court battles. Blackledge said that great consideration was given to the kinds of information the newspaper published:

> *We were trying to ride the fine line between reporting what we thought ought to be reported, and we were trying to be careful not to prejudice the trial.... But we weren't going to let the lawyers edit the newspaper.*[369]

HEARING the HEARING!

Telegraph cartoonist Carl Bieber's take on the Lincoln County judges' gag orders of the press during the Erwin Charles Simants court proceedings. *Bieber family.*

Blackledge was especially proud of *Telegraph* cartoonist Carl Bieber's characterization of the situation. Titled "Hearing the Hearing," the editorial cartoon featured four people, in straitjackets, seated behind the courtroom bar, the word *Press* emblazoned across their chests, tape stretched across their mouths. Bubble thoughts "Hear ye" and "Here come de judge" floated above their heads.

Throughout the ordeal, Blackledge wrote editorials, many of which explained that defending the First Amendment wasn't just for the media—it served the public too. He took the occasional swipe at the magistrates:

> *The Constitution and Bill of Rights did not require that writers or editors or speakers must always be accurate or intelligent. Our Founding Fathers were wise enough to know that would never be so. And they did not set up any such impossible requirements for congressmen or presidents or judges, either.*[370]

Other editorials attempted to rebut rumor and misinformation. When a local attorney suggested that the dispute was merely an effort to sell more newspapers, Blackledge fired off this response:

> *That sort of thing from an attorney is mildly irritating. Especially when it comes at a time when you are trying to calculate whether you can afford the fees for other attorneys to pursue appeals based on the sincere belief by a good many responsible and thoughtful people that principles of free speech and free press must be defended even when the defense is an unpopular one.*[371]

Unpopular indeed. As Blackledge noted years later, "The community generally favored the gag order....The public was willing to sacrifice some press freedoms in order to assure the man convicted of the murders stayed that way."[372]

From the time the original restraining order was issued in the fall of 1975 in an effort to control the dissemination of prejudicial information about the accused, journalists from throughout the country flocked to North Platte. Eventually, the gag orders would trump the news of the deplorable crimes that had been committed.[373] In all, the gag orders, in one form or another, would restrain the press for two and a half months. When the U.S. Supreme Court took up the case, six months had passed. The high court announced the ruling in *Nebraska Press Association v. Stuart* on the last day in June 1976.

Chief Justice Warren Burger, who wrote the opinion, said that rather than trying to control the press, the court could have used other measures to prevent prejudicial information from reaching the public (for example, changing venue, sequestering the jury or delaying the criminal proceedings).[374] Burger also questioned the effectiveness of the restrictive orders: "Pre-trial publicity—even pervasive, adverse publicity—does not inevitably lead to an unfair trial."[375] He continued:

> *We note that the events took place in a community of 850 people. It is reasonable to assume that, without any news accounts being printed or broadcast, rumors would travel swiftly by word of mouth. One can only speculate on the accuracy of such reports, given the generative propensities of rumors; they could well be more damaging than reasonably accurate news accounts. But plainly a whole community cannot be restrained from discussing a subject intimately affecting life within it.*[376]

Although the decision was hailed as a major First Amendment triumph, it fell short of granting the press all it had asked for. Press organizations had wanted an absolutist declaration that no prior restraint of the press could ever be justified in pretrial proceedings given the range of less restrictive alternatives available to the court.[377] Still, the decision is held as one of the Supreme Court's most important decisions in free press/fair trial conflicts.[378] Moreover, it has become the definitive say on the issue: in only the most extreme circumstances can a court impose a prior restraint on the press.[379]

Newspaper publisher Jeff Funk. *Jeff Funk.*

But things were far from being settled in and around North Platte. A little more than a month after the high court's decision in *Nebraska Press Association v. Stuart,* Jeff Funk joined the *Telegraph* as the new courts reporter.[380] It wasn't long before Lincoln County District Court judge Hugh Stuart banned the young reporter from talking to court staff, and staff was prohibited from speaking to Funk. He was not allowed access to court records or calendars. He was banished from the coffee room.

"I was a local courts reporter banned from covering the local courts," declared Funk.[381] Funk said that he'd successfully established relationships with courthouse officials, but not Judge Stuart. Said Funk, "Without realizing it, I was romping around on this still-fresh wound of *NPA v. Stuart.*" Funk said. "Judge Stuart never showed it publicly, but veteran attorneys said the ruling in the case was a stinging blow, harsher because it came from the U.S. Supreme Court and especially because the case bore his name."[382]

Jeff Funk and Judge Stuart were a study in contrasts. While the twenty-three-year-old Funk sported long hair and lamb chop sideburns—fashionable among many young men at the time—Stuart, if not in judicial dress, chose suit and tie as everyday attire. "Stuart expected proper decorum whenever he entered a room. He was powerful, and he commanded respect," the reporter remembered.[383]

Looking back, Funk said that it was easy to see how the clash developed:

> *Like many young journalists of that time, I was a post-Watergate "Wood-*
> *stein" disciple, and I had a degree of skepticism about government and*

people of power or authority. The North Platte courts were new to me, so I looked at a lot of records and asked a lot of questions. A LOT of questions.[384]

Essentially, Stuart had hamstrung Funk's ability to cover an essential chunk of the courthouse beat by blocking the reporter's access to Lincoln County District Court resources—people and documents. Funk turned to his editor for a fix. And the battle lines quickly were drawn between two men of strong convictions: the recalcitrant Judge Stuart and Blackledge, who demanded the restrictions be rescinded.

There is nothing in the research to suggest that the newspaper was ready to take on the censorious judge in another court battle so soon after the high court decision. Rather, the newspaper's local attorney, Don Pederson, finally stepped in to mediate the dispute—Stuart backed down. The young reporter could once again cover the Lincoln County District Court.

Blackledge directly offered Funk a mixture of professional guidance and fatherly advice. As Funk remembers it, the editor told him:

Reporting, like almost every other job up and down Dewey and Jeffers, is about working with people. I was following the rules of journalism without paying attention to the rules of human behavior. I was so caught up in doing my job that I had trampled on the dignity and protocol expected of all.[385]

Funk called Blackledge's advice wise counsel for reporting—and for life:

I returned to the courts beat, stepped up my attire and toned down my bravado. I did better at saying "please" and "thank you," and I worked at observing more and listening more than to just my own questions. I returned to doing good reporting but with a little more diplomacy and maturity.[386]

Funk said that in their limited future contacts, Judge Stuart was cool but professional. However, the rancor between the judge and the editor would endure. And the friction between the judge and the press also would persist as the criminal prosecution of Erwin Charles Simants was following its own tortuous path through the Nebraska court system.

Early in January 1976, just prior to jury selection in Simants's criminal trial in Stuart's courtroom, the judge called together members of the press, whom he asked to voluntarily agree to refrain from publishing certain types of information that might be revealed during the selection process.

Reporters not only refused to sign the agreement, they also boycotted the court session entirely.[387]

On January 17, 1976, jurors convicted Simants on all six counts of the murders of the Henry Kellie family. Judge Stuart sentenced him to death by electrocution. Simants remained on death row for two years after two execution dates were set and stayed.

Then new information unexpectedly came to light. It turned out that Judge Stuart and Lincoln County sheriff Gordon "Hop" Gilster had visited with jurors several times during the trial while they were sequestered in North Platte's Howard Johnson's Motel. Although Stuart's communications with jurors were deemed appropriate, Gilster's not so much. The Nebraska Supreme Court vacated Simants's conviction and death sentence after it concluded that Gilster, a prosecution witness in the trial, had engaged in improper communications with members of the jury, with whom he'd played blackjack and other card games on several occasions.[388] Simants would get a new trial, but this time away from Lincoln County. The trial was moved to Lancaster County in the capital city of Lincoln, Nebraska.

On October 5, 1979, in a courtroom some 250 miles away from the place of the crime and original trial, Simants went on trial for the second time; once more Lincoln County district judge Hugh Stuart presided. For the second time, Simants pleaded innocent by reason of insanity. While this time Judge Stuart refrained from issuing a formal gag on the press, he urged the press to use restraint until a jury could be seated. He also instructed all attorneys involved in the case not to speak to the press. One day shy of the fourth anniversary of the Kellie family murders, on October 17, 1979, the jury found Simants innocent by reason of insanity on all six counts of premeditated murder. Back in Lincoln County, the verdict was met with anger and frustration. Nonetheless, Blackledge reminded readers:

> [The decision] *demonstrated—amply—that a jury in this system can and will return an unpopular verdict....There might be ways to assure more uniformly popular verdicts. A public poll perhaps? Or a town meeting? Any way you dress those methods up, they come out lynch-mob justice. A lynching might have been a popular enough result in this case. But it isn't our system. A jury system certainly will not always bring results that are popular, and not always results that are right. But it is still a system worth preserving.*[389]

In 1979, Simants was committed to the Lincoln Regional Center, where "he likely will remain until he passes away peacefully and quietly, quite unlike the way he dispatched his poor victims in 1975."[390] Under Nebraska law, Simants annually undergoes a review. Thus far, and as recently as early December 2020, the seventy-four-year-old has been denied release. And each year, when Simants's mental status is evaluated, it produces news accounts that resurrect the heinous crimes, as well as the convoluted case culminating in *Nebraska Press Association v. Stuart*.

In the spring of 1980, a press release from the U.S. Army Public Information Office crossed Blackledge's desk. The news: Lincoln County District Court judge Hugh Stuart of North Platte had addressed members of the Twentieth Military Judge Course at the Judge Advocate General's School, U.S. Army, on May 29 in Charlottesville, Virginia.[391] Included was a four-by-six photograph of the judge in a classroom seated before a microphone. Stuart's presentation, attended by trial judges from each of the country's armed services, centered on controlling the media during high-visibility trials. At some point, Blackledge had penned in red across the bottom of the press release, "I can't think of anyone less competent to speak on the subject. His views were unanimously overturned by the U.S. Supreme Court."[392] The press release—with the added sentence written in Blackledge's distinctive hand—and the judge's photo were found among the editor's extensive files relating to the crime and court cases.

Lincoln County district judge Hugh Stuart speaks to students in a military judge course in 1980. *Blackledge Collection.*

THE JUDGE ADVOCATE GENERAL'S SCHOOL, U. S. ARMY
PUBLIC INFORMATION OFFICE
CHARLOTTESVILLE, VIRGINIA 22901

Phone: Area Code 804
293-4333x
293-6885

NEWS RELEASE

RELEASE DATE: __IMMEDIATE__

CHARLOTTESVILLE, VIRGINIA. District Court Judge Hugh Stuart,

Thirteenth Judical District, North Platte, Nebraska, addressed

members of the 20th Military Judge Course at The Judge Advocate

General's School, U. S. Army, 29 May 1980.

Judge Stuart was introduced to the audience by Lieutenant

Colonel Herbert Green, Chief of the School's Criminal Law

Division. In attendance were trial judges from each of the

nation's four services.

Judge Stuart's remarks concerned controlling the press

and mass media during the trial of high visibility cases.

Also addressed were recent developments in this area. The

presentation was very well received, being video recorded

for future use.

NFRC: Sent to:

North Platte Telegraph
North Platte, Nebraska 69101

I can't think of anyone less competent to speak on the subject. His views were unanimously overturned by the U.S. Supreme Court.

Blackledge's opinion about the judge's competency to speak to students about properly conducting trials in high-visibility cases. *Blackledge Collection.*

Back during the time when the gag orders were in place, among the more prominent journalists to visit North Platte was Fred Friendly, former president of CBS news and a professor of journalism at Columbia University.[393] A mutual respect grew between Blackledge and Friendly, who was in North Platte several times doing research for a series about the issue for *The New York Times Magazine*. Later, Blackledge, at the behest of Friendly, went to Columbia University to sit as a panelist on one of the renowned Fred Friendly seminars, "Ethics in America," for public television. Upon the 1976 publication of Friendly's book, *The Good Guys, the Bad Guys, and the First Amendment*, the author sent a copy to his North Platte friend. When Blackledge cracked it open, there on the inside cover was Friendly's personal inscription: "With warm regards and much thanks for helping me to understand the First Amendment in Nebraska."[394]

Chapter 9

THE OLD EDITOR

A reader wishes the old editor would quit referring to himself as the "old editor."
She is kind enough to say he is not so old. Well, that is debatable. What "old
editor" really means is "used-to-be editor." There is a new editor, and he does not
want to be blamed for what I write, nor do I want to take credit for what he writes.
—Keith Blackledge[395]

Shortly before Keith Blackledge retired as executive editor of the *North Platte Telegraph* in 1992, he began referring to himself as the "old editor" in his Sunday "Your Town and Mine" columns. He later explained to readers:

> *I started writing the "Old editor" to avoid the first person singular. Years ago, when I was the editor, an anonymous reader submitted a column of mine with each "I" circled and some sarcastic comment about people who thought they were more important than they were. It is hard to write a personal column without referring to yourself occasionally. At any rate, this writer (notice that's another device to avoid using "I") made a serious effort thereafter to avoid using first person singular when there was another way of phrasing. This often made for awkward sentences, but the writer thought it was worth it.*[396]

He continued:

> *"Used-to-be-editor" is too long and calls for too many hyphens. For some reason, "Retired editor," though accurate, doesn't sound right. "Former*

editor" sounds like someone who might have been fired, or left in a huff, and maybe is still looking for a job. "Old editor" it will have to be.[397]

Neither age nor multiple health challenges would soften or slow the old editor down much. Blackledge wrote his weekly column until his death in 2010, and long after retirement, his involvement in community initiatives and participation in local service organizations would continue.

Blackledge, who suffered from sleep apnea, and his friend and former mayor Jim Whitaker attended the weekly noon North Platte Rotary meetings together for years. Whitaker, who smiled at the recollection, commented that he often had to nudge his tired friend awake. Blackledge once said that he used the time while others slept to plan projects to benefit the town.[398]

There were other health problems too, but Blackledge's wife, Mary Ann, said that diabetes, multiple heart surgeries and the tracheotomy were game changers. "Keith never made a big deal out of his health. He coped with it, and he tried to never let it interfere with his work," she said.[399] A stickler for professional work attire, Blackledge seldom dressed in anything other than a suit or slacks and sport jacket—and a tie. Always a tie. When the breathing device in his throat prevented him from wearing ties, he switched to ascots, many sewn by Mary Ann.[400] In a short story Blackledge wrote some months before his death in tribute to his wife and their marriage, he said, "Their married life together was as happy as a float down the river until he finally became too old to paddle his own canoe, and she had to pull them both over every sandbar."[401]

As the years rolled on, Blackledge's columns sometimes counseled readers. When a popular television commercial promised happiness to young people if they simply went out and did *exactly* what they wanted to do, Blackledge countered:

> *The old editor would recommend to young people that they do some things they don't* exactly *want to do, if only for practice. Sometimes people don't know* exactly *what they want to do. Some people have to find it by trial and error.*[402]

Which is what Blackledge said he did:

> *I never* exactly *wanted to be a writer. It was always hard to get started....I worked a while for a moving company the summer I got out of the Army, and I knew* exactly *that I didn't want to be a heavy lifter. If work was*

Keith and Mary Ann Blackledge. The golden years. *Blackledge family.*

going to be a necessity, newspaper work might be something I could handle. I did think maybe I wanted to be a small town editor. But I had to try big cities once or twice to learn that I was right the first time. I did a lot of others things I didn't exactly *want to do and most ended up bringing good returns in the happiness line.…* [Besides] *it would be a mistake to rely on a television commercial for a philosophy of life.*[403]

Certainly, Blackledge wasn't shy about broaching the subject of age after he retired. After a much younger person asked the old editor what it's like to get old, he attempted the answer in a column. "One of the characteristics of old is the urge to pass along the wisdom of your years. Finding someone willing to listen is a rare occasion," he began. Then followed a list of what he said it feels like to be old:

- *When people start treating you as old. Sometimes they do so out of courtesy.*
- *Sometimes you find a certain indifference you had not noticed before. Store clerks take your money but scarcely look at you. You realize they think of you as too old to possibly be interesting.*
- *Old begins when the doctors, nurses, lawyers, bankers and school teachers look as though they might have just graduated from high school. They surely are too young for such important tasks.*

- *When the waitress seems unreasonably cheerful and talks so fast you have trouble understanding. She probably is young and you probably are old (and irritable).*
- *There is nothing to do about it except ignore it or deny it. "You are only as old as you feel" is a popular but meaningless phrase. A good many old people feel fine but have old attitudes. An equal number feel rotten but stay mentally young. If you feel good when you are old, count it as a bonus. It won't last.*[404]

Blackledge was not without his critics, especially among the more fervent opponents to some of the projects he supported. One such grievance was initiated with a letter to the by-then old editor, from Mike Groene,[405] a fiscal conservative whose opposition to using property tax dollars for community development often put him at odds with Blackledge. When Groene accused the editor of never letting facts get in the way of his personal political views, Blackledge had something to say about fact, fiction, truth and lies:

I have well over half a century in this business. Mike could not know and I cannot count the number of times I have junked a dandy editorial or column when I discovered the facts did not support my position. I have held back stories when I felt the facts needed more checking. I've fired at least two reporters who had trouble separating fact from fiction….Mike closes his letter by saying the promises of politicians and old newspaper editors are "all lies!" That is his opinion, not a fact. I may have guessed wrong sometimes, but I never lied to my readers.[406]

Especially during the later years, Blackledge's columns often reflected a reminiscent mood. In one column, for instance, the old editor wrote about his favorite memories about his sons:

With oldest son Gene, it is the day I took him to sign up for kid-league baseball in Lincoln. When the team coach (former major leaguer Bob Manley) asked each boy what position he would like to play, Gene said "anything but catcher." He was a little timid in those days and didn't speak very loudly. All the coach heard was "catcher," and that was what Gene became. He turned out to have some skill and even more courage in a position that takes more than the average number of bumps and bruises.[407]

Regarding son number two:

Middle son Mark left many indelible memories. One of the most cherished may be the penciled note on a half-sheet of lined yellow notebook paper. It said, "Dad I loved your Editorial. A lot of people have said what a good Editorial. I am proud of you. Mark." Dads don't get compliments like that very often from teenage sons. I still consider it the best editorial award I ever received.[408]

And this about Victor:

Youngest son Vic gave early signs of his competitive drive at one of his birthday parties, probably number five. The race was to see who could be first across the finish line pushing a peanut with his nose. Vic won, and after we wiped the blood from above his upper lip, where he had rubbed the skin off on the carpet, we resolved not to try that game again.[409]

The sons took different career paths, but all are proud of the fact that they write well—a skill they said they'd picked up from their journalism parents.

The eldest, Gene Clayton Blackledge, born on October 8, 1951, is the only son who chose his father's profession. After earning a journalism degree from the University of Nebraska, he covered Nebraska legislative sessions for the Associated Press and later became a bureau correspondent for United Press International in Pierre, South Dakota, Lincoln and Omaha. He ended his career in journalism as a photographer for the NBC affiliate in North Platte and later the ABC affiliate in Omaha. Once during a shoot in a physician's office, he stepped on a scale and noted that he was carrying around seventy-five pounds of equipment. He said he liked the job anyway and continued the work for several more years.[410]

His father's community involvement also rubbed off on Gene. When the city of Minneapolis, where he now resides, allocated funding to revitalize the Stevens Square–Loring Heights neighborhood in downtown Minneapolis, Gene got involved. "We turned this neighborhood around," he declared proudly.[411]

What was it like being the eldest son of Keith Blackledge? "The things that stick with you," he said grinning:

Like when I was painting, dad always said it's the tips of the brush that do the work. Must be a metaphor in that statement somewhere. Or dad's oft-quoted maxim, "Why use a big word, when a little one will do?"[412]

Blackledge surrounded by his three grown sons, *standing, from left*: Gene, Vic and Mark. *Blackledge Collection.*

Gene was in grade school (but he well remembers) when his father snapped a close-up photo of a young calf roping competitor just before the cowboy's horse kicked Blackledge in the face, sending him to the hospital with a concussion and several broken ribs. Gene said he was amazed that some twenty years later people still remembered the accident. By then, Gene, a journalism student at Scottsbluff Junior College, was helping photograph a high school rodeo. "People insisted I set up my camera with a tripod—well out of harm's way."[413]

Among the three, middle son Mark Allan Blackledge stuck closest to home. Mark, born on May 14, 1953, graduated from Ohio State University College of Optometry. He practiced optometry in North Platte for more than thirty years and now has a practice in St. Joseph, Missouri. For Mark, it took until his father got older and frailer for their relationship to deepen. He explained, "I was fortunate those last three years to have had the time and opportunity to reconnect with dad."[414]

During their retirement years, Blackledge and longtime friend Wendell Wood[415] frequently had lunch together at the Airport Café. Mark said after Wood's death in 2009, his father not only missed his old friend, but he also really missed their lunches. That's when Mark decided he'd offer to fill in for Mr. Wood, and before long, the old editor and the optometrist were regulars at the café.[416]

The youngest son, Victor Roy Blackledge, was born on May 22, 1956. Victor (or Vic, as most people call him) looks remarkably like his father. Vic said that when he lost all of his hair following treatment for cancer some years back, he looked like his father's twin. "I couldn't believe it," he said with a laugh.[417]

Vic received his associate degree in mechanical engineering from Normandale Community College in Bloomington, Minnesota. He works in the medical device field, including product development with Cardiovascular Systems Inc. (CSI) in St. Paul, Minnesota. Like his father, the youngest son is a fixer: identifying problems and finding solutions. To that end, Vic holds seven patents for various devices.

He said that North Platte was the perfect community for his father—big enough to handle growth and small enough where one person could make a difference. "Dad was driven by community journalism, and North Platte was fortunate to get him. He would have been a driver wherever he went," he commented.[418] Then, after a long pause, Vic described his father:

> *Dad was a tremendous role model because of his work ethic, his sense of fairness, the way he treated all people. He hated bigotry. He thought all people were worthwhile; you had to prove to him you were not. I have nothing but respect for dad.*[419]

At least once a year, the Blackledges traveled to Colorado or Minnesota, where they fished, camped, hiked, explored. Vic said that he knew he would live in one of those places when he grew up. As it happened, he lived in both, first in Aspen, Colorado, and now, for more than forty years, in Cologne, Minnesota.

Months before Blackledge's death, he and friend John Gale shared their last fly-fishing trip at the Diamond B Trout Resort near Orchard, Nebraska. Sporting waders, vest and favorite cap—Blackledge was going to be fully dressed for this—the old editor fly-fished in between bouts of rest in the cabin or in a chair by the Big Springs Creek, recalled Gale.[420] "He wasn't catching any fish, but he was sure relishing it," Gale said with a sad smile.[421] Gale, former Nebraska secretary of state, and Blackledge had been friends since the early 1970s and fishing buddies for years.

Another lifelong friend was Lavon Sumption, whose relationship with Blackledge got off to a rocky beginning. Sumption arrived in North Platte in 1981 as the new director of the University of Nebraska West Central Research and Extension Center. The fact that the two became friends at all still surprises Sumption.[422]

It seems that a small cadre of citizens—including Blackledge—were opposed to the university's selection of Sumption for the director's job. Some of Blackledge's editorials were especially critical. Sumption was hired anyway. Blackledge later described the friendship:

> *Lavon's welcome to our town was not exactly overwhelming. The trouble was, Sumption failed to cooperate. If you wanted to be unfriendly, you found yourself on a one-way street. There was no answering hostility, anger or resentment. It is a good lesson....Lavon assumed we could work together in spite of my bad attitude, and of course he was right. He assumed we would eventually be friends, and he was right on that, too.*[423]

Sumption also wrote about their friendship—and its shaky beginning—in an opinion piece for the *Telegraph*:

> *Some of us learned the hard way that you never pick a fight with a guy who buys ink by the barrel. So my comments here will be positive....I was prepared not to like this guy Blackledge....Actually, he was the verbose ringleader trying to keep me from getting the job—one of his failed campaigns. I didn't rush to meet him but I saw the respect he commanded and noted the good causes he supported. When I finally met with Keith across his paper-littered desk, asking for his help on a project, he gave me that aloof, skeptical editor's stare for minutes before agreeing to help. The barrier was broken and not over my head.*[424]

Above: During their last fishing trip together in 2010, John Gale (*left*) and Blackledge. *Blackledge family.*

Left: Lavon Sumption. *Lavon Sumption.*

After Sumption left North Platte, their friendship continued. During the last several years of the old editor's life, the spate of e-mails between the two is testament to their mutual regard. Here's one from Blackledge:

> *Our friendship is the richer and our story better for my having been opposed to your appointment....I'm forever indebted to YOU for coming in and breaking the ice. What a lot I would have missed if you hadn't.*[425]

Blackledge received countless local state and national awards—displayed on the walls of his garage. One of the first came in 1958, when the Nebraska Jaycees named Blackledge the state's Outstanding Young Man. Many more tributes would follow and continued long past retirement. Blackledge cherished them all, but he was particularly proud of the Inland Press Association awards for editorial writing because of its connection to William Allen White, the newspaperman he so admired. Other honors included the University of Nebraska Alumni Achievement Award in 1991, the Nebraska Preservation Award from the Nebraska State Historical Society and the Sower Award from the Nebraska Humanities Council, both in 2005, and the Wagonmaster Award at the NEBRASKAland Foundation Statehood Day dinner in 2006.

Blackledge was inducted into the Nebraska Press Association Newspaper Hall of Fame on October 7, 2005. On hand for the standing ovation he received during the ceremony were a number of former *Telegraph* news staffers. The group gathered that weekend in Lincoln for what would be the last of many newsroom alumni reunions.[426]

Then there was Keith Blackledge Day, May 10, 2010. The evening banquet and ceremony included the mayor's proclamation, roasts, toasts and expressions of gratitude. In reference to the Blackledge's desk-side motto— "I wouldn't like to have lived without disturbing anyone"—colleague Eric Seacrest commented, "Keith, I think we have to call you an overachiever." Seacrest continued:

> *Keith, you once admitted that you got caught up in the magic of translating thoughts into words and you didn't want to quit. Let me explain why you kept writing; you kept helping North Platte make progress. Keith, we are glad you didn't retire and take up a hobby like pestering your sons or driving around town excessively slowly leading a parade. Keith, we are glad that rather than pestering just a few people, you decided on a lifelong goal of pestering and prodding everyone.*[427]

Blackledge (*left*) received the Nebraska Press Association Newspaper Hall of Fame Award in 2005. He is pictured with former Nebraska governor David Heineman. *Blackledge Collection.*

Blackledge's response brought the celebration to a close:

> *Newspaper editors are not supposed to have friends. You probably ruined my reputation....But I am grateful....I probably have offended almost everyone here sometime or another, but I have been surrounded by more friends and more opportunities than I ever imagined possible....I have loved this town. I loved the chance to be a part of its history and progress. It has been a great privilege and you have rewarded me more than I deserve.*[428]

Some ten days prior to his death, Blackledge moved to North Platte's Linden Court nursing home. Someone—family, friends, colleagues—seemed to be continuously at his bedside. One of his visitors was photographer George Hipple, who had worked with Blackledge at the *Telegraph*. Hipple said they talked, and then Blackledge asked him to look after Mary Ann:

> *"[E]specially if she has computer problems...or, if she needs a hug every now and then, you make sure you're there." I smiled, agreed and just sat back for a while. Then he looked at me and said, "Hipple, don't you have any work to do? Get out of here—go to work." And that's just the way he was.*[429]

Another visitor was Jim Pappas[430] of Lincoln, who rushed to North Platte because he was alerted that his old friend could pass at any time. But on the day of Pappas's visit, Blackledge did not die. At Pappas's leave-taking, Blackledge apologized for keeping his friend at his bedside for what turned out to be an uneventful day. "That was the kind of guy he was."[431]

Four days before Blackledge died, son Mark rushed to his father's room, where, sitting up in bed, the old editor proclaimed that when he lowered the bed, that would be it—he would be dead. Recalled Mark:

> *Then the nurse came in, took his vitals, and said he's not dying—not today. But dad played with the bed moving it up and down, up and down. Dad was just convinced that when the bed was lowered he would die. But in the end he didn't have that much control. He always had so much control over his life.*[432]

While at Linden Court, Blackledge continued to write by hand what would have been his last column on one of the always-present yellow legal tablets. But when Mary Ann went to type the piece, the tiny scrawl was illegible.[433] According to Mark, "When dad could no longer write, I knew he wouldn't last that much longer."[434]

Blackledge died on July 5, 2010, at 7:18 a.m. Monday morning. He was eighty-three. The previous night, Blackledge and Mary Ann, holding hands, watched from the old editor's room the July 4 fireworks at the fairgrounds.

At the funeral, Blackledge's portrait was flanked by photographs of Jo Ann and Mary Ann. Eric Seacrest delivered the eulogy:

> *Few of us can put the really important things into words. Keith Blackledge certainly could. Keith and his words informed us, encouraged us, fought for us and on occasion chided us....He put his heart and soul into helping his town move forward. And now his heart no longer beats, and we have lost a wonderful friend to us personally and to our town....Keith never had illusions about becoming a writer of great literature. The daily stuff of history told in short, simple sentences was what he hoped for and got.*[435]

As it turned out, Blackledge, while still able to work at his computer, had written one last column. It was published posthumously on July 11, 2010:

> *Did I forget to say "Thanks"? I wasn't ever much good at saying it. My strongest emotion lately has been an overwhelming sense of gratitude for many blessings. Thanks to all those who stopped me in Walmart or elsewhere to say, "I enjoy your column." Thanks to the Seacrest family for*

Keith Blackledge, November 29, 1926–July 5, 2010, North Platte Cemetery. *Heather Johnson.*

lending me their newspaper for so many years. Thanks to staff members who made my job easy. Together we turned out a good community newspaper and had fun doing it.

Thanks to readers who hated something I did or wrote, and forgave me. This town has been remarkably kind and generous. Thanks to Jo Ann, who raised three great boys, and to Mary Ann, who has been the gold in the golden years.

Thanks to true friends. There have been more than I ever thought possible. I don't remember ever being lonely. Thanks to my parents. I didn't know how lucky I was. Thanks for my investment in the future: three boys who grew into good men; the ladies who keep them in line, their children and my two marvelous great-grandchildren. I have been what I was meant to be, done what I was meant to do. Thanks Lord, for that and for all the help I had along the way.[436]

EPILOGUE

Some of the letters to the editor this past year were wise, some were witty, some were outraged, some were confused. Some glowed with appreciation for a good deed by strangers; others groaned with hurt and frustration over some injustice. In short, the letters represented a panorama of the things people think about, the ways they react to events, and the ways they respond to the opinions of others.
—Keith Blackledge[437]

Keith Blackledge made that observation in a column he wrote recapping the newspaper's year in 1978, when the *Telegraph* published 502 letters to the editor—an average of 42 per month. It was a time when people cared about their local newspaper, and the local newspaper cared about the community.

Those days are gone. Newspaper ownership, already in the 1960s, had been shifting from predominantly family-owned to the multimedia conglomerates and newspaper chains. The change—spurred by low interest rates, a prolonged period of economic prosperity and technological innovations— had lowered the cost of producing the paper, meaning newspapers were seen as big moneymakers.[438]

Already by the time Blackledge returned to the *Telegraph* as its executive editor in 1967, newspaper readership was on the decline—first as radio and then television lured readers to a different kind of news. Then along came the Internet—the *Telegraph*'s first e-paper went online in the mid-1990s. To Blackledge, it was an ominous sign.

In a "Your Town and Mine" column written in 2008, Blackledge declared, "The deterioration of newspapers has been caused by owners who push for ever-greater profits without paying attention to the quality of the product they are selling."[439] He warned that sloppy journalism and a generation of reporters and editors who can't spell and don't seem to care were hurting newspapers generally and the *North Platte Telegraph* particularly.

The column was followed by a scorching letter to the paper's management in which Blackledge reproached the executives for publishing

> *a two-column picture of a famous comedian with a cutline that says he is recovering and will be dismissed from the hospital Saturday morning, running with a long story and fairly large headline about his death that day…a picture of three people at the Golden Spike with only two identified. The third was the visitor who came to present the award, wife* [Rhonda Seacrest] *of a former owner of this newspaper.*[440]

Blackledge's tirade continued:

> *Incomprehensible to me is using a routine house fire in Sargent, almost out of our territory, as the lead story in a Tuesday paper four days after the event. There apparently was no embarrassment about the time element, since it stated in the headline that this took place on Thursday. I hope someone raised holy hell about that.*[441]

Thus, by 2008, while Blackledge was lamenting the shoddy quality of the *North Platte Telegraph*, consolidation in the industry had been going on for some time, and corporate chains increasingly were shutting down papers.

The succession of ownership of the *North Platte Telegraph* throughout the years illustrates the larger story of an industry in transition—and trouble.

When Blackledge came to the *Telegraph* in 1967 to head the news department, the J.R. Seacrest publishing family recently had purchased the paper and several others in the state. In 2000, the *Omaha World-Herald* bought the Seacrest operation. And in 2011, a year after Blackledge's death, Berkshire Hathaway (BH Media Group) purchased Warren Buffett's hometown newspaper, the *Omaha World-Herald*, and twenty-seven other dailies in the state, including the *Telegraph*.

Fans of local print newspapers might have taken some comfort by Buffett's words:

Newspapers continue to reign supreme in the delivery of local news. If you want to know what's going on in your town—whether the news is about the mayor or taxes or high school football—there is no substitute for a local newspaper.[442]

But by 2017, Buffett had changed his tune. For the past several years, the company saw advertising revenue dip precipitously, following the national trend, while increasing subscription prices further exacerbated reader exodus. For example, between 2015 and 2017, BH Media's print circulation decreased 15 percent. And from 2000 to 2015, overall print newspaper advertising revenue dropped from some $60 billion to $20 billion.[443]

Early in 2018, BH Media implemented system-wide staff reductions affecting nearly 150 people and eliminating some 100 vacant positions at its newspapers. Later that year, Lee Enterprises of Davenport, Iowa, took the management reins of all the Berkshire Hathaway–owned daily newspapers—including the *North Platte Telegraph*. More staff reductions followed.[444] Early in 2020, Lee Enterprises purchased BH Media Group.

What had happened? As Americans increasingly were going online for more of their news, newspaper companies were ramping up their digital content as a strategy for long-term survival—often to the detriment of the print product. Between 2004 and 2018, some 1,800 newspapers closed as numbers of people buying print papers plunged.[445] Meanwhile, the industry continued to adapt by providing online news options, but the digital advertising barely kept news organizations afloat.[446]

The changing landscape for news consumption has had sobering repercussions not only for the print newspaper business but also for the communities they serve. In a 2018 study titled "The Expanding News Desert," University of North Carolina researchers from the School of Media and Journalism's Center for Innovation and Sustainability in Local Media found that local news is cratering nationwide. Consider:

- More than 1,400 towns and cities in the United States have lost a newspaper in the last fifteen years.
- Nearly 200 of the 3,143 counties in the United States no longer have a newspaper.
- The number of independent owners and family-owned newspapers has declined significantly in recently years.
- The largest twenty-five newspaper chains own one-third of all newspapers, including two-thirds of the country's 1,200 dailies.[447]

Corporate ownership means that decisions about individual newspapers and their communities are made by owners without a direct stake in the outcome. Corporate ownership means the quest for profits trumps the traditional print newspaper's civic mission, which is to hold local officials accountable, provide readers with a connection to their communities and deliver reliable news for an informed local citizenry.[448]

During the time the *Telegraph* was under the umbrella of the *Omaha World-Herald*, Blackledge already was concerned about the threat posed to local news. As he wrote to *Telegraph* management in 2008, "Stories only of interest in Omaha are being published in the North Platte paper just as they appear in the *World-Herald*—sometimes with the same headline." He also chided the executives for not taking the time and skilled desk work to make the newspaper's parenthood less obvious. With that, the letter closed, "I canceled my subscription to the *World Herald* earlier this year because I could read most of it in the *Telegraph*."[449]

Then, in early 2020, along came the Covid-19 pandemic, and things got a lot worse for local newspapers as advertising revenue continued to plummet. Yet—the irony—news consumption was up for first time in a long time as the coronavirus gripped the country. According to a series of Knight Foundation/Gallup surveys, attention to local news had doubled since December 2019 as a diminishing cadre of journalists across the country scrambled to cover the impact of the pandemic—for despite the readership surge, newsrooms continued to cut staffs and paychecks.[450]

By the spring of 2020, a number of media trackers had reported that hundreds of journalists—many among the Lee Enterprises chain—had been laid off or furloughed. The prediction: more layoffs were almost a certainty in the coming weeks and months.[451]

Moreover, roughly one in four newspapers in the country have closed since 2004, while most industry watchers predict that hundreds more could close—an extinction-level event that likely would hit the smaller newspapers as well as ones that are part of the huge chains.[452]

The fates of these newspapers, including Blackledge's beloved *Telegraph*, remain to be seen. Certainly, optimists hope that the need for local information about a serious public health crisis will rekindle interest in reading local news.

Whatever the future holds for the industry, Blackledge's career merits renewed attention. His legacy, found in the thousands of editorials and columns he wrote spanning nearly fifty years, offers lessons about how community journalism worked in a small midwestern town. Additionally,

Blackledge authored three books—he often referred to them as slim volumes—that provide insight into his town and its past. *A Short History of North Platte and the Election of 1951* was published in 2005; *Letters Home*, a compilation of letters he wrote to his family during his military service, in 2008; and *That Town Fights about Everything* in 2009.

When *A Short History* was published, Ed Howard, former Nebraska Associated Press political reporter, both praised—and ribbed—the editor:

> *Blackledge has long admired tell-it-like-it-is journalism. In that spirit, some truth should be told about him. The fact is that Keith Blackledge has always been completely lacking in some characteristics that Hollywood movies attributed to many scribes of his generation. Examples: No one has ever told a story about Blackledge being lamppost-hugging drunk while simultaneously trying to interview a fire hydrant at 3 a.m. He has never learned to swear worth a damn. And there is no public record of Blackledge knocking down a shot of rye or a mouthy advertiser with the speed of Bogart winking at Bacall. Still, Blackledge compensated for those deficiencies. He ran a good newsroom…and used a keyboard like a community cattle prod to help accomplish much that was good. And he has pointed out more than a few things that were bad. Blackledge would be a worthy subject for a "slim volume" himself someday.*[453]

NOTES

Prologue

1. Keith Blackledge, "Personal Thoughts about Being an Editor," *North Platte Telegraph*, December 9, 1990.
2. Dan Moser first came to the *Telegraph* in 1983. He was a general news reporter and also covered the courts and city hall. He became managing editor in 1989 and in 1991 succeeded Keith Blackledge as executive editor.
3. Dan Moser, interview by author, Lincoln, NE, September 4, 2014.
4. Bill Eddy became a general assignments reporter at the *Telegraph* in 1972. He was the assistant editor for several years until leaving the paper in 1979. From that time until his retirement in 2011, he held city, business and special editions editorships at the *Lincoln Journal/Journal-Star*.
5. Sharron Hollen began writing obituaries and weather part time at the then *Telegraph-Bulletin* in 1960. Two years later, she was a full-time reporter, retiring in 2010. At the time she started at the paper, she was the only woman in the newsroom. Throughout the years, Hollen wrote the popular "Reporter at Large" column.
6. John Martinez joined the *Telegraph* news staff in 1966. He died on July 16, 1991.
7. The *Bieber Cartoon* was a regular Saturday feature on the *Telegraph* opinion page from 1970 to 1976. The cartoon was suspended when Bieber became mayor and resumed for a time in the 1980s. Bieber died on May 31, 1993.

8. Keith Blackledge, interview by Chuck Salestrom, North Platte, NE, January 25, 2010.
9. Keith Blackledge, "Thoughts about the Changes in Society, and in Newspapers," *North Platte Telegraph*, April 14, 1996.
10. Keith Blackledge, "Old Dogs, New Tricks, but Learning," *North Platte Telegraph*, January 22, 1984.
11. Keith Blackledge, "More than a Sports Editor," *North Platte Telegraph*, July, 21, 1991.
12. Combs and Burbul, "Historic Downtown North Platte, Nebraska."
13. Ibid.
14. Keith Blackledge, "A Subservient Right Is No Right at All," *North Platte Telegraph*, October 23, 1975.
15. Claussen and Shafer, "On Community Journalism," 3–7.
16. Mary Ann Blackledge, interview by author, North Platte, NE, February 6, 2014.

Chapter 1

17. Newspaper clipping found in the personal papers of Keith Blackledge. No title, date or author provided.
18. Blackledge's father, Victor, was in the newspaper business throughout his life. After Keith left home, his father also co-owned the *Chadron (NE) Record*. He died on December 7, 1971, in Scottsbluff.
19. Keith Blackledge, "On Being a Great-Grandfather," *North Platte Telegraph*, January 13, 2007.
20. Blackledge, *Things I Wish My Father Had Told Me*, 33.
21. Polly Blackledge died on May 20, 1983, in Gering, NE.
22. Walter Blackledge, e-mail interview by author, February 5, 2013. Walter Blackledge earned a master's degree from William Allen White School of Journalism at the University of Kansas. For years he was on the editorial staff of the Lindsay-Schaub newspapers in Decatur, Illinois.
23. Keith Blackledge, "Memories of Favorite Teachers," *North Platte Telegraph*, February 24, 1985.
24. Ibid.
25. Blackledge, *Things I Wish My Father Had Told Me*, 66.
26. Ibid., 14.
27. Keith Blackledge, "My First Journalistic Venture," *North Platte Telegraph*, March 6, 2005.

28. Ibid.

29. Blackledge, *Things I Wish My Father Had Told Me*, 54.

30. Ibid., 164.

31. Walter Blackledge e-mail interview.

32. Blackledge, "Memories of Favorite Teachers."

33. Keith Blackledge, "Teachers in the Business of Touching Lives," *North Platte Telegraph*, November 29, 1977.

34. Ibid.

35. Blackledge, *Things I Wish My Father Had Told Me*, 66.

36. John G. Neihardt, born in 1881, was an American writer and poet. *Black Elk Speaks*, published in 1932, is his best-known work. The Nebraska legislature established the position of poet laureate in 1921 when it named Neihardt as the first state designee. Neihardt served a lifetime appointment. He died in 1973.

37. Keith Blackledge, "A Good Poet to Know as well as Read," *North Platte Telegraph*, January 29, 1978.

38. Blackledge, "Teachers."

39. Blackledge, "Memories."

40. Blackledge, *Things I Wish My Father Had Told Me*, 67.

41. Ibid., 66.

42. Keith Blackledge, "Recollections of a Bench Warmer," *North Platte Telegraph*, November 13, 1983.

43. Keith Blackledge, "Life Lessons that Stick with You," *North Platte Telegraph*, June 5, 2005.

44. Ibid.

45. Ibid.

46. Blackledge, *Things I Wish My Father Had Told Me*, 78.

47. Ibid., 79.

48. Ibid., 59.

49. Ibid., 98.

50. Ibid., 109.

51. For a personal account of Blackledge's military experience and the time he spent in the Philippines, see his compilation of letters to his family in *Letters Home*, published in 2008.

52. Blackledge, *Things I Wish My Father Had Told Me*, 118.

53. Keith Blackledge, "Remembering Train Rides of War Years, and 50 Years Later," *North Platte Telegraph*, September 10, 1995.

54. Keith Blackledge, "Please Give Them Good Care, We May Want Them Returned," *North Platte Telegraph*, August 4, 1979.

55. Daryl Hall, "All Are Fine, I Think," *Scottsbluff Star-Herald*, August 8, 1979.
56. Ibid.

Chapter 2

57. Keith Blackledge to Victor Blackledge, June 12, 1946, in *Letters Home*, 130–32.
58. Blackledge, *Things I Wish My Father Had Told Me*, 124.
59. Ibid., 132.
60. Ibid., 65.
61. Blackledge was one of seven U.S. Air Force unit members at the University of Missouri designated "Distinguished Military Student." He tied with another MU student for the highest score in the nation in the ROTC armament course tests. He received his commission as a second lieutenant, United States Air Force Reserve, on June 3, 1949.
62. Blackledge, *Things I Wish My Father Had Told Me*, 138.
63. Ibid., 147.
64. American Presidency Project, "Harry S. Truman."
65. Blackledge, *Things I Wish My Father Had Told Me*, 147.
66. Ibid.
67. Ibid., 158.
68. Dubbed the "Subway Series" between the two New York City professional baseball teams, the 1951 World Series was the last for Joe DiMaggio, who retired afterward, and the first for rookies Willie Mays and Mickey Mantle.
69. Blackledge, *Things I Wish My Father Had Told Me*, 160.
70. Ibid., 174.
71. Robert Dole represented Kansas in Congress from 1961 to 1996. He served in the U.S. Senate from 1984 to 1996. He was the Republican Party's vice presidential nominee in the 1976 presidential election and the presidential nominee in 1996. Dole was born and raised in Russell, and it remained his official place of residence throughout his political career.
72. Blackledge, *Things I Wish My Father Had Told Me*, 175.
73. Ibid.
74. Ibid.
75. Ibid.
76. Kirk Mendenhall was mayor of North Platte from 1951 to 1953. He had been a North Platte Chamber of Commerce director in the 1940s and 1950s. He died at the age of eighty-one on August 18, 1994, in North Platte.

77. William "Bill" Jeffers, born in North Platte in 1876, also was known as the "Rubber Czar" for coordinating production of rubber for the government during World War II. He began work for Union Pacific Railroad after graduating from high school. When he was named president of UP in 1937, a community-wide event celebrated his rise from a railroad call boy to company president. He died on March 6, 1953, in Pasadena, California.

78. The Missouri River flood was caused by higher-than-usual March temperatures that followed a long and snowy winter in the Midwest in 1952. Some eighty-seven thousand people were displaced, and the damages were estimated at nearly $180 million.

79. Nebraska Department of Roads and Irrigation Program and Planning Section, "Report of an Origin and Destination Survey North Platte, Nebraska."

80. In 1948, at a cost of $3.5 million, the Union Pacific Railroad built the first large, modern classification yard in North Platte where train cars are pushed over a hump and sorted into new trains according to destination. The eastbound hump, the Bailey Yard, was completed in 1968 at a cost of $12.5 million.

81. Keith Blackledge in a typed note, dated May 13, 2008.

82. Keith Blackledge, "Let Me Tell You About Our Town," *North Platte Telegraph*, August 13, 1987.

83. Wishart, *Encyclopedia of the Great Plains*, n.d.

84. Ibid.

85. Community History Archive of the North Platte Genealogical Society, n.d.

86. Keith Blackledge, "Thoughts about Changes in Society and in Newspapers," *North Platte Telegraph*, April 14, 1996.

87. Famed Pony Express rider, army scout, buffalo hunter and showman William F. "Buffalo Bill" Cody spent his most productive adult years in North Platte.

88. This local history was found in undated typed notes in Keith Blackledge's papers. Other Blackledge documents indicate an ongoing research of North Platte's history that often found its way in the editor's columns and editorials.

89. While a census of cities and towns with two newspapers does not exist, it is safe to say such places are continuing to dwindle. It's unclear how many smaller communities like North Platte have both daily and weekly publications, although it's a safe bet there aren't many.

90. Keith Blackledge, "Some Deep and Moving Thoughts," *North Platte Telegraph*, November 15, 1968.

91. Keith Blackledge, "Old Dogs, New Tricks, but Learning," *North Platte Telegraph*, January 22, 1984.

92. Ibid.

93. Blackledge, *Things I Wish My Father Had Told Me*, 178.

94. Jim Kirkman was at the *Telegraph* for 50 years. He began as a sports editor while still in high school, then went on to work full time as the sports editor and advertising manager. He was the newspaper's publisher from 1968 until his retirement in 1976. He served as North Platte's mayor from 1984 to 1992. Kirkman died on January 7, 1999, at the age of eighty-eight. Kirkman and Blackledge remained friends throughout their lifetimes.

95. Blackledge, *Things I Wish My Father Had Told Me*, 178

96. Joe di Natale started in radio in 1935, working for stations in Lincoln, NE, and joining station KODY in North Platte in 1938. The sports broadcaster died in 1987. Posthumously, he was inducted into the Nebraska High School Sports Hall of Fame in 1999. In 1994 Blackledge received the Joe di Natale Award from the North Platte Jaycees.

97. Blackledge, *Things I Wish My Father Had Told Me*, 178.

98. "Jazz King Was a Youngster Here," *North Platte Telegraph-Bulletin*, February 24, 1954.

99. Keith Blackledge, "Seeing the Town after 35 Years," *North Platte Telegraph*, May 26, 1991.

100. Harry Contos's joined the *Telegraph-Bulletin* news staff in 1950 after graduating from Western Michigan University. He earned his law degree from Notre Dame in 1959 and practiced law in Kalamazoo, Michigan, from 1959 until his retirement. He died in Kalamazoo on April 11, 2010, at the age of eighty-four. Contos and Blackledge were lifelong friends.

101. Blackledge, "Seeing."

Chapter 3

102. Blackledge, "Thoughts about Changes."

103. Ted Turpin—a Chadron, NE native—met Blackledge when the two were on the news staff at the *North Platte Telegraph-Bulletin*. Following Blackledge, Turpin served as managing editor of the paper. After North Platte, he was an agricultural reporter for the *Wall Street Journal* and

a columnist for the *Tucson (AZ) Daily Citizen*. He later owned a small weekly newspaper and several real estate magazines. Turpin died on December 17, 2016.

104. Keith Blackledge to Ted Turpin, March 17, 1960.

105. Keith Blackledge to Ted Turpin, August 20, 1960.

106. Keith Blackledge to Ted Turpin, October 11, 1960.

107. Blackledge to Turpin, October 11, 1960.

108. Ibid.

109. Blackledge to Turpin, August 20, 1960.

110. Ibid.

111. Keith Blackledge to Ted Turpin, November 16, 1960.

112. Al Neuharth was an assistant managing editor at the *Miami Herald* for a time. He went on to start *USA Today* in 1982. With its unique design and colorized graphics and photos, *USA Today* eventually changed the look of newspapers everywhere.

113. The date the *North Platte Herald* ceased publication is unknown. If someone took the paper on after the Weimer brothers' departure, it is not chronicled.

114. Blackledge to Turpin, August 20, 1960.

115. Blackledge to Turpin, October 11, 1960.

116. Keith Blackledge to Claytons (no first names), September 17, 1960.

117. Keith Blackledge to Wendell Wood, October 17, 1960.

118. Blackledge to Turpin, November 16, 1960.

119. Keith Blackledge to Ted Turpin, February 2, 1961.

120. Keith Blackledge to Ted Turpin, May 3, 1961.

121. Blackledge to Turpin, February 2, 1961.

122. Blackledge to Turpin, May 3, 1961.

123. Ibid.

124. Ibid. Note that many letters to Turpin were written over the course of several days, even weeks.

125. Blackledge to Turpin, February 2, 1961.

126. Ibid.

127. Keith Blackledge to Victor and Polly Blackledge, May 25, 1961.

128. Keith Blackledge, interview by Chuck Salestrom, North Platte, NE, January 10, 2010.

129. As a teenager, Erma Bombeck worked as a copygirl for the *Dayton Herald*. She joined the *Journal Herald* on the women's desk in 1949. Drawing on her role as wife and mother, her column found humor in family life. She died on April 22, 1996.

130. Clement Vallandigham, a leader of the Ohio Democratic Party, was an opponent of the American Civil War. The lawyer-politician's career ended abruptly on June 17, 1871, when, preparing the defense of an accused murderer, Vallandigham enacted his version of events at the crime scene. Not realizing that the pistol he was using as a prop was loaded, the attorney pointed it at himself and pulled the trigger. Vallandigham was mortally wounded. He is buried at Woodland Cemetery in Dayton.

131. James Middleton Cox served in the U.S. House of Representatives, had twice been the governor of Ohio and was the Democratic nominee for president of the United States in 1920. He retired from public office to focus on his chain of newspapers, Cox Enterprises, which today includes newspapers, radio, television and social media enterprises.

132. Keith Blackledge, "Ideological Labels Misleading," *North Platte Telegraph*, June 8, 1986.

133. Ibid.

134. Ibid.

135. Blackledge interview by Salestrom, January 25, 2010.

136. Blackledge, "Ideological Labels Misleading."

137. Blackledge, *Short History of North Platte and the Election of 1951*, back cover.

Chapter 4

138. Blackledge, "Personal Thoughts about Being an Editor."

139. William Allen White's editorial ridiculing Kansas for economic stagnation, titled "What's the Matter with Kansas?" captured national attention.

140. See, for example, Terry, "Community Journalism Provides Model for Future," 71–83; Griffith, *Hometown News*, 159–60.

141. Blackledge, "Let Me Tell You about Our Town."

142. Keith Blackledge, "A Note of Thanks to W.A. White," *North Platte Telegraph*, February 24, 1977.

143. Joe R. Seacrest to Keith Blackledge, November 3, 1966.

144. Keith Blackledge, "Whether the Editor Was Right or Wrong, a Promise Was Kept," *North Platte Telegraph*, April 2, 1995.

145. Rick Ruggles, "It's Hard to Believe Now, but the Oakland Raiders and Denver Broncos Played a 1967 Preseason Game in North Platte, Nebraska," *Omaha World Herald*, August 27, 2017.

146. Colburn, *From Picas to Bytes*, 19–36.

147. Ibid., 147.

148. In 1968, Joe R. and James C. Seacrest changed the name to Western Publishing Company.

149. Jim Seacrest, interview by author, Lincoln, NE, July 15, 2014.

150. Jim Seacrest and his wife, Rhonda, lived in North Platte from 1968 to 2000, when they moved to Lincoln. They were renowned throughout Nebraska for their philanthropy. Jim Seacrest died on June 2, 2016.

151. Colburn, *From Picas to Bytes*, 120–27.

152. Keith Blackledge, "Something New for Us and You," *North Platte Telegraph*, June 10, 1968.

153. Keith Blackledge, "Some Things Change, and Some Things Stay the Same," *North Platte Telegraph*, August 21–22, 1976.

154. Keith Blackledge, "On Publishing amid the Wreckage," *North Platte Telegraph*, October 16, 1968.

155. Ibid.

156. Keith Blackledge, "Slings and Arrows," *North Platte Telegraph*, August 4, 1968.

157. Keith Blackledge, "Advance Notice Might Be Useful," *North Platte Telegraph*, September 9, 1968.

158. Keith Blackledge, interview by Chuck Salestrom, North Platte, NE, January 25, 2010.

159. Jim Seacrest interview.

160. Blackledge, "Whether the Editor."

161. Harold Kay practiced law in North Platte from 1954 to 2007. His legal strategy and arguments in Lincoln County are credited for ensuring that the Nebraska Press Association's appeal of Lincoln County restrictive orders was heard by the U.S. Supreme Court. Kay died on September 23, 2014.

162. Keith Blackledge, "Board of Education Needs Commitment to Open Meetings," *North Platte Telegraph*, September 7, 1984.

163. Ibid.

164. Keith Blackledge, "Response Not Warranted by Editorial," *North Platte Telegraph*, July 11, 1984.

165. Harold Kay, interview by author, Lincoln, NE, March 7, 2013.

166. Jim Seacrest interview.

167. The Inland Press Association is a nonprofit organization for member newspapers from throughout the United States, Canada and Bermuda. Now America's Newspapers, its mission is to support and promote the newspaper industry.

168. Jim Seacrest interview.

169. Blackledge, "Personal Thoughts about Being an Editor."

170. Terry, "Community Journalism Provides Model for Future," 77–78.

171. Eric Seacrest, interview by author, North Platte, NE, May 15, 2014.

172. Ibid.

173. Judy Nelson, interview by author, Lincoln, NE, March 5, 2015.

174. Sharron Hollen, interview by author, North Platte, NE, May 15, 2014.

175. Jill Claflin, interview by author, North Platte, NE, November 11, 2014

176. Jill Claflin walked into the *Telegraph* office one day in 1980 to complain to the editor about the paper's coverage of a trial. Keith Blackledge listened to her complaint and offered her a job. She began as a copy editor on weekends. She was back at the *Telegraph* as executive editor from 1993 to 1996, when she became an editorial manager for Habitat for Humanity national in Atlanta, GA. She retired in 2014.

177. Moser interview.

178. Ibid.

179. Ibid.

180. Dan Moser, "FAA Official: Bid Lacked Key Requirement," *North Platte Telegraph*, December 2, 1983.

181. Moser interview.

182. Keith Blackledge, "Not All Things to Everyone, but Aiming to Inform," *North Platte Telegraph*, October 15, 1983.

183. McCombs and Shaw, "Agenda-Setting Function of Mass Media," 176–87.

184. David Swartzlander, "Retired *Journal* Editor Downplays Personal Power," *Lincoln Journal Star*, April 20, 1986.

185. Mark Blackledge, "A Better Place Because He Called It Home," *North Platte Telegraph*, July 11, 2010.

Chapter 5

186. Blackledge, "Personal Thoughts about Being an Editor."

187. Colburn, *From Picas to Bytes*, 54.

188. Blackledge, "Better Place Because He Called It Home."

189. Keith Blackledge in a typed note, dated December 3, 2007, found in his personal papers.

190. Ibid.

191. Ibid.

192. In 1960, Allen Strunk succeeded his father, Harry, as publisher of the *McCook Gazette*, which started as a weekly in 1911. The paper became a daily in 1924 and was sold in 1986.

193. Blackledge, *This Town Fights about Everything*, 33.

194. Ibid., 45–48

195. Ibid., 36.

196. Ibid., 45–48.

197. Ibid.

198. Keith Blackledge, "Mid-Plains Moves Ahead in Spite of Obstacles," *North Platte Telegraph*, December 15, 1967.

199. Blackledge, *This Town Fights about Everything*, 1–8.

200. Keith Blackledge, "The Prejudice that Blinds," *North Platte Telegraph*, January 29, 1973.

201. Bill Eddy, interview by author, Lincoln, NE, October 9, 2014.

202. Chuck Salestrom, interview by author, North Platte, NE, November 15, 2012.

203. Hollen interview.

204. Blackledge, *This Town Fights about Everything*, 79–84.

205. Ibid.

206. Keith Blackledge to David Patton, 1997.

207. Blackledge, *This Town Fights about Everything*, 82.

208. Keith Blackledge, "County Museum and Heritage Center Is 20 and Still Growing," *North Platte Telegraph*, March 10, 1996.

209. Blackledge, *This Town Fights about Everything*, 64.

210. Ibid., 75–78.

211. Keith Blackledge, "Canteen Story Never Fails to Move; Spirit Lives on After 50 Years," *North Platte Telegraph*, October 12, 1994.

212. Ibid.

213. Greene, *Once Upon a Town*, 263.

214. *North Platte Telegraph*, "Wild West Show Dream Come True: Years of Study, Preparation Yield Goal for Show's Producer," July 31–August 1, 1971.

215. "Lassie Stars Out West," Buffalo Bill's Wild West Show, press release, n.d.

216. Gary Toebben was president of the North Platte Chamber of Commerce from 1975 to 1981. His friendship with Blackledge continued long after Toebben left North Platte. Toebben became president of the Los Angeles Area Chamber of Commerce in 2006. He retired on July 1, 2018.

217. Gary Toebben, e-mail interview by author, March 18, 2014.

218. Keith Blackledge, "Grand Island Makes a Good Thing of Railroad We Lost," *North Platte Telegraph*, January 25, 1977.

219. Ibid.

220. Frank Graham, "Golden Spike Isn't NP's First Big Idea to Draw Scorn," *North Platte Bulletin*, June 15, 2005.

221. Ibid.

222. Mark Blackledge, interview by author, North Platte, NE, May 15, 2014.

223. Keith Blackledge, "Agreeing to Disagree on '30s Building," *North Platte Telegraph*, June 13, 2003.

224. Jim Whitaker, interview by author, North Platte, NE, February 6, 2014.

225. Blackledge, *Short History of North Platte and the Election of 1951*, 31–54.

226. Keith Blackledge, "Good Rules for Any Life," *North Platte Telegraph*, January 24, 1993.

227. Whitaker interview.

228. Jim Whitaker graduated from North Platte High School, the University of Nebraska and the University of Denver College of Law. He returned to North Platte in 1963, when he became the owner-operator of Whitaker Furniture. Whitaker and Blackledge were involved in many of the same community campaigns. Whitaker died on June 7, 2017, in North Platte.

229. Whitaker interview.

230. Ibid.

231. Ibid.

232. Keith Blackledge, "Landscaping East Fourth a Needed Project," *North Platte Telegraph*, May 3, 1985.

233. Jim Seacrest interview.

234. Keith Blackledge, "Revisiting a Search for Facts on the Past of Cody Park Carousel," *North Platte Telegraph*, February 18, 1996.

235. Sharron Hollen, "Cody Park Carousel Now Has Band Organ," *North Platte Telegraph*, May 22, 2004.

236. Keith Blackledge, "Now If We Could Get Music for City's Carousel," *North Platte Telegraph*, April 8, 1989.

237. Hollen, "Cody Park."

238. North Platte native John Gale served as Nebraska's secretary of state from 2000 to 2018. He and Blackledge met while both worked on the campaign to merge the two North Platte hospitals. Their friendship endured.

239. John Gale, interview by author, Lincoln, NE, October 21, 2014.

240. Keith Blackledge, typed notes, testimony before the Nebraska Legislative Education Committee, 1989, found among his personal papers.

241. Rodney Bates served as director of television and general manager of KUON-TV at the University of Nebraska and director at NET Foundations.

242. Rodney Bates, interview by author, Lincoln, NE, May 15, 2014.

243. Ibid.

244. Gale interview.

245. Ed Howard became the capitol correspondent for the Associated Press in Lincoln in the mid-1970s. In later years, he wrote for the Nebraska Statepaper website. He died on June 5, 2012, in Lincoln.

246. Ed Howard, "A Small Book about North Platte from One with a Big Love for the City," August 1, 2005, previously available at NebraskaStatePaper. com. Website is re-launching as nebraska.statepaper.com.

Chapter 6

247. Blackledge, "Personal Thoughts about Being an Editor."

248. Mary Ann Blackledge interview.

249. This scenario was repeatedly described by interviewees who worked with Blackledge in the *Telegraph* newsroom.

250. Keith Blackledge, "Fantasizing: If the Editor Ran This City," *North Platte Telegraph*, May 15, 1988.

251. Keith Blackledge, "Letter from the Editor: Your Town…and Mine," *North Platte Telegraph-Bulletin*, April 28, 1958.

252. Keith Blackledge, "Letter from the Editor: Your Town…and Mine," *North Platte Telegraph-Bulletin*, November 3, 1958.

253. Keith Blackledge, "Letter from the Editor: Your Town…and Mine," *North Platte Telegraph-Bulletin*, September 21, 1957.

254. Keith Blackledge, "Letter from the Editor: Your Town…and Mine," *North Platte Telegraph-Bulletin*, April 15, 1959.

255. Keith Blackledge, "A Year of Sundays," *North Platte Telegraph*, September 11, 1978.

256. Keith Blackledge, "Attitudes about Birthdays Do Improve," *North Platte Telegraph*, December 6, 1992.

257. Keith Blackledge, "Letter to a Young Man," *North Platte Telegraph*, November 28, 1973.

258. Keith Blackledge, "Life's Perspective from Age 60," *North Platte Telegraph*, November 30, 1986.

259. Keith Blackledge, "An Old Editor's Views on Old Age," *North Platte Telegraph*, November 19, 2006.

260. Keith Blackledge, "Succinct Resolutions for Editor," *North Platte Telegraph*, December 30, 1984.

261. Keith Blackledge, "Wine, Letters and Other Tidbits," *North Platte Telegraph*, May 8, 1981.

262. Keith Blackledge, "Freedom of Speech and Headaches," *North Platte Telegraph*, January 18, 1987.

263. Ibid.

264. Keith Blackledge, "A Morning Telegraph," *North Platte Telegraph*, July 1, 1979.

265. Eric Seacrest interview.

266. Blackledge, "Morning Telegraph."

267. Eric Seacrest interview.

268. Keith Blackledge, "Dear Ann: They Like You Better than Me," *North Platte Telegraph*, August 21, 1979.

269. Mary Ann Blackledge interview.

270. Keith Blackledge, "A Centennial Year in Review," *North Platte Telegraph*, January 1, 1982.

271. Ibid.

272. Keith Blackledge, "A Real Conversion Process," *North Platte Telegraph*, October 28, 1982.

273. Keith Blackledge, "International Incident Avoided," *North Platte Telegraph*, January 10, 1982.

274. Ibid.

275. Ibid.

276. American Presidency Project, "Remarks to Citizens in North Platte, Nebraska."

277. Keith Blackledge, "No Dull Week, Even without the President," *North Platte Telegraph*, August 12, 1987.

278. Keith Blackledge, "Reagan's Return Sets a Record for Our Town," *North Platte Telegraph*, August 24, 1990.

279. Keith Blackledge, "Stage Star's Grandfather Doctored Buffalo Bill," *North Platte Telegraph*, January 13, 1991.

280. Keith Blackledge, "Looking Very Closely at Opportunities that May Deserve a Revival," *North Platte Telegraph*, October 10, 1993.

281. Keith Blackledge, "There's Bieber, Along with Others of the Best," *North Platte Telegraph*, April 22, 1976.

282. Ibid.

283. Keith Blackledge, "More than a Sports Editor," *North Platte Telegraph*, July 21, 1991.

284. Ibid.

285. Ibid.

286. David Anderson to *Telegraph* news staff reunion participants, August 18, 1994.

Chapter 7

287. Keith Blackledge, "The Newspaper and Its Readers Helped Educate Our Family," *North Platte Telegraph*, September 4, 1994.

288. Moser interview.

289. Ibid.

290. David Anderson to *Telegraph* news staff reunion participants, August 18, 1994.

291. Keith Blackledge, "Two of the Best Move to New Jobs," *North Platte Telegraph*, September 9, 1990.

292. David Anderson to Mary Ann Blackledge, July 5, 2010.

293. David Anderson worked as a political reporter before earning his law degree. He taught media law and First Amendment law at the University of Texas School of Law and lectured at universities in Australia, England, Sweden, Italy and the Netherlands. He retired in 2018. His memoir, *An Urn of Native Soil*, was published in 2014. He and Blackledge were lifelong friends.

294. David Anderson, e-mail interview by author, February 11, 2013.

295. David Anderson to Mary Ann Blackledge.

296. Hollen interview.

297. Ibid.

298. Sharron Hollen, interview by author and Chuck Salestrom, North Platte, NE, July 12, 2014.

299. Nelson interview.

300. Judy Nelson went on to publish nine works of fiction, which she describes as Jane Austen 1820s comedy romance novels.

301. Nelson interview.

302. Keith Blackledge, "Judy Shows What It Takes to Be a Writer," *North Platte Telegraph*, October 8, 1989.

303. Hollen interview.

304. Nelson interview.

305. John DeCamp served in the Nebraska legislature from 1971 to 1987. He died in Norfolk, NE, on July 27, 2017, at the age of seventy-six.

306. In the 1984 Republican state primary for the U.S. Senate, Nancy Hoch defeated her five male challengers, and the Nebraska City native came within 4 percentage points of defeating the Democratic incumbent, U.S. Senator J. James Exon.

307. Dan Moser, "DeCamp Assails 'Party Bosses,' Says Mrs. Hoch 'Shallow on Issues,'" *North Platte Telegraph*, April 28, 1984.

308. Moser interview.

309. Ibid.

310. Blackledge, "Two of the Best."

311. Anderson e-mail interview.

312. David Anderson to Mary Ann Blackledge.

313. Keith Blackledge, "Floating Down the River: A Short Story," unpublished manuscript, February 2010.

314. Ibid.

315. Jo Ann Blackledge taught journalism at North Platte High School from 1968 to 1987. She advised both the student newspaper and yearbook. Throughout her teaching career, she was active in the Nebraska High School Press Association and in 1981 was named a Distinguished High School Journalism Adviser. She and Keith Blackledge divorced in 1992.

316. Keith Blackledge, "Teachers Who Left a Legacy," *North Platte Telegraph*, April 29, 2007.

317. At Blackledge's urging, George Hipple joined Habitat for Humanity in 1999. He was an international photographer and traveled the world for the organization until 2014. He is owner and operator of George Hipple Photography in North Platte.

318. George Hipple, interview by author and Chuck Salestrom, North Platte, NE, July 12, 2014.

319. Peggy Woodruff, interview by author and Chuck Salestrom, North Platte, NE, July 12, 2014.

320. Mary Hepburn, interview by author and Chuck Salestrom, North Platte, NE, July 12, 2014.

321. Mary Hepburn wrote for various publications and was a journalism teacher and later a writer for the National Institutes of Health in Bethesda, Maryland.

322. Keith Blackledge, "One of Our Graduates Is Writing for Us Once Again…in a New Way," *North Platte Telegraph*, March 3, 1996.

323. Rodney Wenz remained connected to North Platte. In 2003, he helped with fundraising for improvements to the World War II Canteen exhibit at the Lincoln County Historical Museum. He died on November 19, 2008.

324. Mary Ann Blackledge interview.

325. Beginning in 1990, Jill Claflin headed the news operation at the *Lexington Clipper-Herald*, where she started the free monthly Spanish newspaper *Qué Pasa*. She was the executive editor of the *North Platte Telegraph* from 1993 until 1996, when she became editorial manager for Habitat for Humanity in Atlanta, GA. She retired in 2014.

326. Jill Claflin, interview by author, Kearney, NE, July 11, 2014.

327. Gale interview.

328. Ibid.

329. Tom Osborne—a Hastings, NE native—served in the U.S. House of Representatives from Nebraska's Third Congressional District from 1973 to 1997.

330. Gale interview.

331. Ibid.

332. After North Platte, Gary Toebben went on to head the Lawrence, Kansas Chamber, and the North Kentucky Regional Chamber, covering thirty-nine cities, and before retiring in 2018, he was president of the Los Angeles Area Chamber.

333. Toebben e-mail interview.

334. Bob Greene, "Ringside Reporter," *North Platte Telegraph*, December 20, 1980.

335. Keith Blackledge, "A Letter from the Editor to Bob Greene," *North Platte Telegraph*, December 23, 1980.

336. Ibid.

337. Bob Greene, "Ringside Reporter," *North Platte Telegraph*, January 9, 1981.

338. Bob Greene, e-mail interview by author, February 25, 2015.

339. Bob Greene, *Once Upon a Town*, 264.

Chapter 8

340. Blackledge, "Subservient Right."

341. Eddy interview.

342. Ibid.

343. *North Platte Telegraph*, "Hearing Set Wednesday in Mass Murder," October 20, 1975.

344. Ibid.

345. *Omaha World Herald* photograph titled "Latent Fingerprint Evidence. Note Left by Simants," found in Blackledge papers, n.d.

346. *North Platte Telegraph*, "Hearing Set Wednesday in Mass Murder."

347. Fred Friendly, "Judges Wrestle with Fair Trial-Free Press Issue," *New York Times*, March 23, 1976.

348. Eddy interview.

349. *North Platte Telegraph*, "Hearing Set Wednesday in Mass Murder."

350. For a thorough discussion of the crime and the legal conflict, see Mark Scherer, *Rights in the Balance: Free Press, Fair Trial, and Nebraska Press Association v. Stuart* (Lubbock: Texas Tech University Press, 2008).

351. Friendly, "Judges Wrestle."

352. Ibid.

353. Eddy interview.

354. Jim Seacrest interview.

355. Harold Kay practiced law in North Platte for fifty-three years from 1954 to 2007, during which time he and Blackledge sparred on occasion. He died on September 23, 2014.

356. Eddy interview.

357. Ibid.

358. Kay interview.

359. Ibid.

360. "Star chamber" is a pejorative term that reflects the doubt cast on the legitimacy of secret court proceedings common in the English court of law in the late fifteenth and early sixteenth centuries.

361. Friendly, "Judges Wrestle."

362. Keith Blackledge, "The Press and the Courts," *North Platte Telegraph*, October 29, 1975.

363. Media of Nebraska, a consortium of print and broadcast media outlets in Nebraska, handled the collection and distribution of funding for the litigation.

364. Blackledge, "Subservient Right."

365. Friendly, "Judges Wrestle."

366. Kay interview.

367. Jim Seacrest interview.

368. Bill Eddy, "Judge Orders New Restrictions on Press," *North Platte Telegraph*, October 28, 1975.

369. Russomanno, *Speaking Our Minds*, 260.

370. Keith Blackledge, "Of Congress Courts and NFO," *North Platte Telegraph*, December 19, 1975.

371. Blackledge, "Press and the Courts."

372. Berens, "Prior Restraint Threatens Free Speech."

373. Kay interview.

374. *Nebraska Press Association v. Stuart,* 427 U.S. 539 (1976), 555.

375. Ibid., 554.

376. Ibid., 567.

377. Kay interview.

378. Whitmore, "Nebraska Suppressed," 107–22.

379. Other types of restraints, including suppressing press access to trail participants (referred to as indirect gag orders), still create secrecy and controversy.

380. Jeff Funk has been a newspaperman for some forty years, serving as editor, digital director or publisher in Nebraska, Kansas and Oklahoma. He currently is publisher of the *Enid (OK) News & Eagle.*

381. Jeff Funk, e-mail interview by author, February 16, 2016.

382. Ibid.

383. Ibid.

384. Ibid.

385. Ibid.

386. Ibid.

387. *North Platte Telegraph,* "Court Reopens, but Reporters Decline Judge's Limitations," January 6, 1976.

388. *North Platte Telegraph,* "The Crime that No One Can Forget," *North Platte Bulletin,* October 19, 2005.

389. Keith Blackledge, "Not Designed to Be Popular," *North Platte Telegraph,* October 31, 1979.

390. Dan Moser, "Erwin Charles Simants and the System: How to Balance All Interests Fairly?" *North Platte Telegraph,* July 16, 1993.

391. Judge Hugh Stuart retired on March 1, 1986, as Lincoln County district judge after some twenty-one years in North Platte to become an administrative law judge with the Social Security Administration in Omaha. He died on April 3, 2002, in Omaha.

392. Judge Advocate General's School, U.S. Army Public Information Office, "News Release," May 1980.

393. Fred Friendly, a pioneer in television news, was a strong defender of the First Amendment and advocated for robust news coverage on public television. He died on March 3, 1998.

394. Friendly, *Good Guys, the Bad Guys, and the First Amendment,* front inside cover.

Chapter 9

395. Keith Blackledge, "Old Editor Answers a Handful of Complaints," *North Platte Telegraph*, February 1, 1998.

396. Ibid.

397. Ibid.

398. Whitaker interview.

399. Mary Ann Blackledge interview.

400. Ibid.

401. Blackledge, "Floating Down the River."

402. Keith Blackledge, "Trying to Find Happiness," *North Platte Telegraph*, January 11, 1998.

403. Ibid.

404. Keith Blackledge, "Age Is More than a State of Mind," *North Platte Telegraph*, June 22, 2008.

405. Republican Mike Groene of North Platte held strong anti-spending views that often resulted in high-profile fracases within his own party and with the Democrats. He was elected to the Nebraska legislature in 2014.

406. Keith Blackledge, "Facts, Opinion and the Truth," *North Platte Telegraph*, March 14, 2010.

407. Keith Blackledge, "Life Lessons that Stick with You," *North Platte Telegraph*, June 5, 2005.

408. Ibid.

409. Ibid.

410. Gene Blackledge, interview by author, Minneapolis, MN, August 2, 2014.

411. Ibid.

412. Ibid.

413. Ibid.

414. Mark Blackledge interview.

415. Wendell Wood's friendship with Blackledge dates back to the 1950s, when Blackledge first wrote for the paper. They worked together on numerous community endeavors. He died on March 8, 2009.

416. Mark Blackledge interview.

417. Victor Blackledge, interview by author, Plymouth, MN, August 1, 2014.

418. Ibid.

419. Ibid.

420. Gale interview.

421. Ibid.

422. Lavon Sumption, interview by author, Lincoln, NE, May 12, 2015.

423. Keith Blackledge, "It's Hard to Stay Unfriendly if Foe Won't Reciprocate," *North Platte Telegraph*, December 3, 1995.

424. Lavon Sumption, "A Special Thanks to the Old Editor," *North Platte Telegraph*, November 20, 2006.

425. Keith Blackledge to Lavon Sumption, November 26, 2006.

426. Mary Ann Blackledge interview.

427. Eric Seacrest, transcript of Keith Blackledge Night.

428. Keith Blackledge, transcript of Keith Blackledge Night.

429. Hipple interview by author and Salestrom, July 12, 2014.

430. Jim Pappas is the former president of the North Platte Pork Producers organization. He was a Nebraska senator from 1983 to 1987 and worked with Blackledge on numerous community initiatives.

431. Jim Pappas, interview by author, Lincoln, NE, May 12, 2015.

432. Mark Blackledge interview.

433. Mary Ann Blackledge interview.

434. Mark Blackledge interview.

435. Eric Seacrest, transcript of funeral eulogy.

436. Keith Blackledge, "The Old Editor Writes -30- One Last Time," *North Platte Telegraph*, July 11, 2010.

Epilogue

437. Keith Blackledge, "Your Opinion Has a Place on This Page," *North Platte Telegraph*, January 28, 1979.

438. Alex S. Jones, "And Now the Media Mega Merger," *New York Times*, March 24, 1985, https://www.nytimes.com.

439. Keith Blackledge, "Newspapers Are Killing Themselves," *North Platte Telegraph*, August 17, 2008.

440. Keith Blackledge to Job, Peter, Pat, *Telegraph* editors, August 20, 2008.

441. Ibid.

442. Mamta Badkar, "Buffett Explains Why He Paid $344 Million for 28 Newspapers, and Thinks the Industry Still Has a Future," *Business Insider*, March 1, 2013, http://www.businessinsider.com.

443. Derek Thompson, "The Print Apocalypse and How to Survive It," *The Atlantic*, November 3, 2016. https://www.theatlantic.com.

444. "Buffett Taps Lee Enterprises to Manage Many of his Berkshire Newspapers," CNBC, June 26, 2018. https://www.cnbc.com.

445. Adam Gabbatt, "U.S. Newspapers Face 'Extinction Level' Crisis as Covid-19 Hits Hard," *The Guardian*, April 9, 2020. http://www.theguardian.com; Steve Jordon and Brad Davis, "*Omaha World-Herald* Eliminates 43 Jobs, Makes Changes to Newspaper," *Omaha World-Herald*, February 21, 2018, https://www.omaha.com.

446. Gabbatt, "U.S. Newspapers."

447. Penny Abernathy, "2018 Report: The Expanding News Desert," UNC-Chapel Hill Research, November 25, 2018, https://www.usnewsdeserts.com.

448. Ibid.

449. Blackledge to Job, Peter, Pat.

450. Zacc Ritter, "Amid Pandemic, News Attention Spikes; Media Favorability Flat," Knight Foundation, April 9, 2020, https://knightfoundation.org.

451. See, for example, Kristin Hare, "Here Are the Newsroom Layoffs, Furloughs and Closures Caused by the Coronavirus," Poynter Institute, April 29, 2020, www.poynter.org, and Noah Kirsch, "Tracker: Media Layoffs, Furloughs and Pay Cuts Due to Coronavirus," *Forbes*, April 6, 2020, https://www.forbes.com.

452. Gabbatt, "U.S. Newspapers."

453. Howard, "Small Book about North Platte."

BIBLIOGRAPHY

American Presidency Project. "Harry S. Truman: Commencement Address at the University of Missouri," June 9, 1950. http://www.presidency.ucsb.edu

———. "Remarks to Citizens in North Platte, Nebraska, August 13, 1987." Ronald Reagan XL President of the United States: 1981–1989. University of California at Santa Barbara. http://www.presidency.ucsb.edu.

Anderson, David. Letter to Mary Ann Blackledge, Austin, Texas, July 5, 2010.

———. Letter to *North Platte Telegraph* news staff reunion participants, Austin, Texas, August 18, 1994.

Berens, Charlyne. "Prior Restraint Threatens Free Speech." *University of Nebraska College of Journalism & Mass Communications Alumni News*, 2001. http://journalism.unl.edu.

Blackledge, Keith. Letter to Claytons (no first names), Miami, September 17, 1960.

———. Letter to David Patton, North Platte, NE, 1997.

———. Letter to Job, Peter, Pat, North Platte *Telegraph* editors, North Platte, August 20, 2008.

———. Letter to Ted Turpin, Miami, August 20, 1960.

———. Letter to Ted Turpin, Miami, February 2, 1961.

———. Letter to Ted Turpin, Miami, March 17, 1960.

———. Letter to Ted Turpin, Miami, May 3, 1961.

———. Letter to Ted Turpin, Miami, November 16, 1960.

———. Letter to Ted Turpin, Miami, October 11, 1960.

———. Letter to Victor and Polly, Miami, May 25, 1961.

———. Letter to Wendell Wood, Miami, October 17, 1960.

———. *Letters Home.* North Platte, NE: Old 101 Press, 2008.

———. *A Short History of North Platte and the Election of 1951.* North Platte, NE: Lincoln County Historical Society, 2005.

———. *Things I Wish My Father Had Told Me.* North Platte, NE: self-published, 2006.

———. *This Town Fights about Everything.* North Platte, NE: Enterprise Inc., 2009.

Claussen, Dane, and R. Richard Shafer. "On Community Journalism." *Grassroots Editor* 83, no. 3 (1997): 3–7.

Colburn, Faith. *From Picas to Bytes: Four Generations of Seacrest Newspaper Service to Nebraska.* North Platte, NE: Prairie Wind Press, 2013.

Combs, H. Jason, and Derrick Burbul. "Historic Downtown North Platte, Nebraska: Historic Buildings Survey." Nebraska State Historic Preservation Office of the Nebraska State Historical Society, Fall 2009. https://archive.org.

Community History Archive of the North Platte Genealogical Society. N.d. http://northplatte.advantage-preservation.com.

Friendly, Fred. *The Good Guys, the Bad Guys, and the First Amendment.* New York: Random House, 1976.

Greene, Bob. *Once Upon a Town: The Miracle of the North Platte Canteen.* New York: Harper Collins, 2002.

Griffith, Sally. *Hometown News: William Allen White and the Emporia Gazette.* New York: Oxford University Press, 1989.

Judge Advocate General's School, U.S. Army Public Information Office. "News Release." Charlottesville, VA, May 1980.

McCombs, Maxwell, and Donald Shaw. "The Agenda-Setting Function of Mass Media." *Public Opinion Quarterly* 36, no. 2 (Summer 1972): 176–87.

Nebraska Department of Roads and Irrigation Program and Planning Section. "A Report of an Origin and Destination Survey North Platte, Nebraska." Department of Commerce, with Department of Commerce Bureau of Public Roads, March 1954. http://govdocs.nebraska.gov/epubs/R6000/B044.5215-1954.pdf.

Russomanno, Joseph. *Speaking Our Minds: Conversations with the People behind Landmark First Amendment Cases.* Mahwah, NJ: Lawrence Erlbaum Associates, 2002.